INDIAN FEMINISMS

This book is dedicated to all the activists in the Indian
feminist movements – for their efforts to make a difference...

Indian Feminisms
Law, Patriarchies and Violence in India

WITHDRAWI

GEETANJALI GANGOLI
University of Bristol, UK

ASHGATE

© Geetanjali Gangoli 2007

Published by
Ashgate Publishing Limited
Gower House
Croft Road
Aldershot
Hampshire GU11 3HR
England

Ashgate Publishing Company
Suite 420
101 Cherry Street
Burlington, VT 05401-4405
USA

Ashgate website: http://www.ashgate.com

British Library Cataloguing in Publication Data
Gangoli, Geetanjali
   Indian feminisms : law, patriarchies and violence in India
   1. Feminism - India - History 2. Women - India - Social
   conditions 3. Women - Legal status, laws, etc. - India
   I. Title
   305.4'2'0954

Library of Congress Cataloging-in-Publication Data
Gangoli, Geetanjali.
   Indian feminisms : law, patriarchies, and violence in India / by Geetanjali Gangoli.
     p. cm.
   Includes index.
   ISBN-13: 978-0-7546-4604-4 (alk. paper) 1. Feminism--India. 2. Family violence--
Law and legislation--India. 3. Women--Legal status, laws, etc.--India. 4. Sex and
law--India. I. Title.

   HQ1742.G36 2007
   305.420954--dc22

2006031459

ISBN-13: 978-0-7546-4604-4

Printed and bound in Great Britain by MPG Books Ltd, Bodmin, Cornwall.

Contents

List of Abbreviations

AMM	Annapurna Mahila Mandal
APL	Above Poverty Line
APRM	Anti-Price Rise Movement
AWM	Autonomous Women's Movements
BJP	Bhartiya Janata Party
BPL	Below Poverty Line
CITU	Centre of Indian Trade Unions
Congress (I)	Congress (Indira)
CPI (ML)	Communist Party of India (Marxist Leninist)
CPI	Communist Party of India
CPIM	Communist Party of India Marxist
Cr.P.C	Criminal Procedure Code
DD	Dying Declaration
FAOW	Forum Against Oppression of Women
FAR	Forum Against Rape
FIR	First Investigation Report
HMA	Hindu Marriage Act
IEA	Indian Evidence Act
IPC	Indian Penal Code
IWM	Indian Women's Movement
JMS	Janwadi Mahila Samiti
LABIA	Lesbians and Bisexuals in Action
LBT	Lesbian, Bisexual and Transgendered
MP	Member of Parliament
MPL	Muslim Personal Law
NCW	National Commission for Women
NFIW	National Federation of Indian Women
OBC	Other Backward Castes
PIL	Public Interest Litigation
PITA	Immoral Traffic in Women and Children (Prevention) Act
PUDR	People's Union of Democratic Rights.
RSS	Rashtriya Seva Sangh
SAB	Sexual Assault Bill
SITA	Suppression of Immoral Traffic (in Women)Act
SMA	Special Marriages Act
TADA	Terrorists and Disruptive Activities (Prevention) Act

UCC	Uniform Civil Code
UN	United Nations
WDP	Women's Development Programme
WGWR	Working Group on Women's Rights

Glossary

Agni Pariksha: Trial by fire.

Awaaz-e-Niswaan: Literally, the voice of women; feminist organisation working predominantly with Muslim women in Mumbai.

Bindi: The holy dot or *bindi* is an auspicious makeup worn by young Hindu girls and women on their forehead, and is traditionally a red dot made with vermilion, and signifies female energy (*shakti*) and is considered a symbol of marriage.

Brahmin: Person belonging to the highest hindu caste of the varna system of traditional hindu society, and regarded to be responsible for society's spiritual aspects. A man born into a Brahmin family becomes twice-born (dvija) when he undergoes initiation into Vedic education.

Dalit: *Dalit* in Sanskrit is derived from the root *dal* which means to split, break, crack, used first by social reformer Jotiba Phule (1827–1890), to describe the outcastes and untouchables as the oppressed and broken victims of the Indian caste-ridden society. Used in contemporary India to describe 'Sudras'.

Dharma: In Hindu philosophy, 'dharma' means religious duty. In Buddhism 'dharma' implies 'protection' from suffering by following Buddha's teachings.

Harijan: The polite form for *untouchable* coined by Mahatma Gandhi literally 'people of God', however this term is considered condescending and Dalit is preferred.

Iddat: Islamic custom, wherein, upon the husband's death, or divorce or annulment of the marriage by some other manner, the woman has to remain confined in one house for a specified period of time. In case of divorce, she has to observe 'iddat' till she has three consecutive menstrual periods, or if she is pregnant, until the child is born.

Janwadi Mahila Samiti: Democratic Women's Organisation, attached to the Communist Party of India (Marxist).

Kali: Hindu goddess, known for her role as destructor of evil, a non-benign form of Goddess Parvati, wife of Shiva. Kali is worshipped nationally, but especially in Eastern India, and has also been used as a feminist icon.

Khanawali: Literally, provider of food, used by women cooking commercially for working class men.

Kshatriya: Person belonging to the warrior caste, derived from *kshatra*, meaning 'dominion, power, government'.

Latni: Rolling pin.

Lok Sabha: Literally House of the People; similar in composition to the House of Commons in the UK, therefore made up of elected representatives from all over the country.

Mahila Atmaraksha Samiti: Women's Self Defence Organisation.

Mangalsutra: Literally 'auspicious thread', it is a string of black beads worn by married Hindu women, a symbol of matrimony.

Mehr: Mehr refers to a sum of money, or property that is agreed by a husband and wife at the point of marriage, payable to the woman at any agreed point during the marriage. If the marriage breaks down due to desertion, divorce or death, the husband is liable to pay the wife the agreed mehr.

Morcha: Popular demonstrations and agitations against a specific cause.

Narmada Bachao Andolan: Literally, Save River Narmada Movement. It is a national coalition of environmental and human rights activists, scientists, academics, and project-affected people, working to stop several dam projects in the Narmada Valley.

Naxalite: An informal name given to revolutionary communist groups that were born out of the Sino-Soviet split within the Indian communist movement. The term comes from Naxalbari, a village in West Bengal where a leftist section of (CPI(M)) led a militant peasant uprising in 1967, to establish 'revolutionary rule' in India.

Nikaahnama: Used in Islamic marriage, and is a contract between the couple that can include the fixing of the mehr amount, conditions for divorce etc.

Panchayats: Local self-government bodies, primarily at village levels.

Saptapadi: The 'saptapadi' refers to a specific ritual central to Brahminical marriages that is based on seven steps taken around a sacred fire, each step signifying a vow made between the couple, blessed by the priest solemnizing the ceremony.

Sati: An upper caste Hindu custom in India in which the widow was burnt to ashes on her dead husband's pyre; also used to describe a virtuous woman.

Shakti: Literally strength, also another name for Kali.

Shri: Hindi word for Mr.

Smt.: Short for Shrimati, or Mrs.

Stree Jagruti Samiti: The Forum of Women Awakening.

Sudra: Member of the fourth and lowest caste, his role in Vedic India was that of an artisan or a labourer, also the 'untouchable' caste that have suffered various forms of oppression.

talaq-e-biddat: Literally improper Talaq, includes pronouncing more than one Talaq in a single menstrual cycle. If a person pronounces such a Talaq it is considered effective while the man is considered guilty of severe sin.

Talaq: Literally dismissal, but under Muslim Personal Law, it means divorce.

Thana: Police station.

Vaishya: Member of the third of the four major castes comprising of merchants, artisans and landowners.

Varna: Caste, literally means 'colour'.

Acknowledgements

This book is based on research conducted on the Indian feminist movements between 1993 to the present. I am grateful for a number of friends and colleagues in encouraging me to start the work, persevere with it, and finally to publish it.

In Delhi, I thank Janaki Abraham, Pratiksha Baxi, Shahana Bhattacharya, Uma, Anand and Anuja Chakravarti, Nivedita Menon, Ranjana Padhi, Sumit and Tanika Sarkar for academic support and friendship.

In Bombay I am grateful to my 'Forum' friends, especially Nandita Gandhi, Sandhya Gokhale, Sujata Gothoskar, Ramlath Kavil, Nandita Shah and Gopika Solanki and Seema Kazi, from the Women's Research and Action Group, all of whom never stopped challenging me, and helping me develop my ideas.

In the UK, I thank colleagues at the Violence Against Women Research Group, University of Bristol including Gill Hague, Marianne Hester, Ellen Malos, Melanie McCarry and Nicole Westmarland. A special word of gratitude is due to Michelle Kelly Irving, who has read and commented on several chapters. I am also grateful to Mary Savigar and Carolyn Court and other colleagues at Ashgate Publishing Ltd for showing confidence in my work, and for their patience and help.

Finally, I would like to acknowledge with gratitude, the support and love of my family – my parents, Usha and Mohan; my brother, Nikhil; my sister's family, Raju, Nandita, Unnati and Minoti and my husband, Martin. They all kept me going, and this book would not have been possible without them.

Chapter 1

Introduction

Introduction

Feminist movements in India have posed challenges to established patriarchal institutions such as the family, and to dominant social values and structures, most significantly in the arena of legal interventions in the areas of violence against women. Feminists have intervened in the area of law in at least three ways. One, to expose the working of patriarchal controls and structures within law, for instance, critiquing civil marriage and divorce laws that extend more rights to men than women. Two, to unpack the plural ways in which law operates, including offering some redress to women in situations of domestic violence and finally, to campaign to extend rights to women, such as campaigns against sexual assault and rape. As a movement that has challenged hegemonic notions of the 'Indian family', detractors have constructed Indian feminism as a distinctly western phenomenon. Therefore Indian feminists have been forced to confront and combat claims of being 'westernised' both from the state and from sections of civil society, including by right wing Hindu fundamentalist forces as being alienated from the 'Indian' realities of family structures.

This book will address the global relevance of concepts such as 'patriarchy' and 'feminism' and feminist interpretations of 'local' issues and patriarchies through the study of Indian feminism from the 1970s to the present. To this end, it will examine and analyse feminist campaigns on issues of violence and women's rights, and debates on the possible ways in which feminist legal debates may be limiting for women, and could possibly be based on exclusionary concepts such as citizenship. It will also look at the strengths and limitations on working on law reform for feminists. I will also look at whether legal feminisms relating to law and women's legal rights are effective in the Indian context. The book will examine whether legal campaigns lead to positive changes in women's lives or whether they further legitimise oppressive state patriarchies. The book will also look at the recasting of caste and community identities, specifically the rise of Hindu fundamentalism, and the ways in which feminists in India have combated and confronted these challenges.

This introductory chapter will set the terms of the debates that will be addressed in the book. I will begin by a short summary on the economic and social 'status' of women in contemporary India, followed by examining the main issues that will be tackled in the book, and the methodology used while conducting the research on which this book is based. I will then examine the relationship between 'western' and 'Indian' feminisms; debates within Indian feminism on law and rights and challenges posed to Indian feminism from Hindu fundamentalist forces and globalisation.

Women's 'Status' in India

Scholars agree that it is very difficult to measure the 'status of women' especially in the context of a large and diverse country such as India (see for instance: Devi 1993; Kishor and Gupta 2004). While women in India theoretically enjoy a number of legal rights, in practice these are denied to them. The Fundamental Rights incorporated in the Indian constitution include equality under the law for men and women (Article 14), equal accessibility to the public spaces (Article 15), equal opportunity in matters of public employment (Article 16), equal pay for equal work (Article 39). In addition there are statutory provisions that guarantee these rights, such as the Equal Remuneration Act of 1976 and the Maternity Benefit Act, 1976. The Dowry Prohibition Act, 1961 prohibits the giving and taking of dowry, and Section 498 A Indian Penal Code, 1983, criminalises physical and mental cruelty to married women perpetuated by their husbands or in laws. Under the Hindu Succession Act, 1955, Hindu women were granted equal rights to parental self-acquired property in the case of intestate succession, but not ancestral property. Widows had an absolute right over affinal property (Kishwar 1993). However, under an amendment made to the Hindu Succession Act in 2005, Hindu women have been extended equal coparcenary rights to ancestral property. However the Act still allows parents to disinherit daughters in the case of self acquired property through the use of a will.

Studies have suggested that variables including women's access to education, the media and paid employment are some economic pointers to women's status, while participation in decision making, age at marriage, extent of, social and personal acceptance of domestic violence, and women's mobility are social indicators (Kishor and Gupta 2004). While some Indian women have attained prestigious posts in the judiciary, education, politics, IT, medicine and other myriad fields, these benefits are denied to the majority of women in the country. National data demonstrates that proportions of women working for cash are low in most states in India (ranging from 49 per cent in some states to 10 per cent in others), as is women's freedom of movement and access to the public sphere more generally. Only one in three women can go to the market without permission from their family, and one in four visit friends and relatives without permission. Women have less education than men, with only just over 50 per cent of the female population in India being literate, as compared to 75 per cent of the male population. Not surprisingly therefore, women enter marriages much earlier than men, and marry men who are both older and more educated than themselves (Kishor and Gupta 2004). The average age for marriage for women in India is 12.6 years (UN 1998), therefore suggesting that child marriages are common in different parts of the country. Most women have limited participation in decisions about their lives including visiting their natal families, health care, and making expensive purchases. National data also reveals that one in five women have experienced some form of violence from their husbands, or other members of their families since age 15, and there is a high degree of acceptance of domestic violence among women, with 57 per cent of married women aged between 15–49 accepting that a man is justified in beating his wife if she does not fulfil accepted gender roles including cooking, neglecting the home, or if her natal family do not provide the expected dowry (Kishor and Gupta 2004). Dowry demands at marriage are a part of Indian marriages, while dowry was once a Hindu upper caste custom; it has become a part of the marriage customs of different castes and communities. Dowry demands have been conceptualised as one of the reasons leading to son preference (Sunder Rajan 2003), leading to female infanticide and sex pre-selection and abortion of female foetuses, therefore leading to the sex ratio, which in contrast with western societies, favours men to women with 927 women per 1000 males in the 1991 census (CEDAW 2002). The 1991 census marks the trend of the continuing and what has been called 'a secular decline in the sex ratio from the beginning of the last century' (Krishnaji 2001).

As we will see later in this chapter, structural factors such as caste, community and class status impact on women's access to rights, and freedom from violence as have socio-economic developments related to globalisation in the 1990s. For instance, poverty and other forms of social deprivation have been found to be the single most important reason that women in India enter the sex trade, which has been seen as an area of concentrated violence against women in the trade (Pandey et. al. 2003). It has been suggested that women's inferior position in India is due to their lack of control over arable land, and research has indicated a gap between owning land (which some women do) and controlling land (which very few women do); and also found that although some laws grant women rights over land, local practice often thwarts the exercise of those rights (Aggarwal 1994). In addition, women in India have often limited access to mainstream political power and studies have found tenuous links between feminist movements and the political interests of women parliamentarians (Rai 1995).

Structure and methodology

Structure of the book

This book will look at the ways in which feminists in India have impacted legal and social debates on women's rights, violence against women and sexuality. Chapter 2 examines a brief survey of feminist history and activism both nationally, and in the city of Mumbai (Bombay until 1992), which has been an important centre of feminist – and more generally radical politics, including a vibrant trade union movement. This chapter will discuss the emergence of feminism in the 1970s and 1980s; where the exigencies of post colonial Indian politics manifested themselves in the form of the excesses of the Emergency (1974–76); and the influence of nationalist and socialist politics. I will examine how, in spite of a recognition of the patriarchal limits of the organised Left, the feminist movement, given its ideological closeness to these groups, could not but take up issues relating to working class women, rather than middle class women.

Chapter 3 looks at the ways in which feminists have conceptualised and influenced the gendered aspects of the debates on citizenship and women's rights, through an examination of the limitations of the notion of citizenship for women. While Indian feminists have often argued that women in India have rights equal to men because they are Indian citizens, the State constructs the female citizen as notionally equal within the constitution but legally men and women have different rights. This chapter will examine these issues through the debates on minoritised Muslim women and sex workers.

Chapter 4 traces the varied ways in which criminal and civil laws in India construct women's sexuality. A range of criminal and civil laws will be analysed from this perspective, including laws on rape, prostitution, maintenance, adultery, divorce, homosexuality and pornography, and I will assess whether there is a continuum between criminal and civil law as far as the construction of women's sexuality is concerned. Feminist responses to, and impacts on these debates will be looked at. Chapter 5 will examine the feminist anti-rape campaign beginning in the 1980s on the issue of custodial rape, through legislative debates; judicial interventions and feminist challenges to mainstream ideas of 'custodial' rape. I will analyse the strengths and limitations of feminist theorisations on rape, and the ways in which feminist paradigms have shifted from the 1980s to the early twenty-first century.

Chapter 6 analyses the overlap between the State and feminist discourses on dowry and on domestic violence. Through a study of legislative debates, judicial statements, police rhetoric and feminist statements I will look at the implications of negating the differences between these two often distinct forms of oppression. This chapter will also look at the links between communalisation and domestic violence. The concluding chapter will bring together some of the themes discussed in the previous chapters and offer some conclusions on whether law is indeed a 'subversive site' for feminists (Kapur and Cossman 1996), or whether feminist justice is indeed impossible within law (Menon 1995b). The chapter will also offer conclusions on the relationship between western and Indian feminisms by showing how Indian feminists both 'borrow' from and contribute to western feminisms. Finally, the book will offer some insights into the challenges posed by caste and communal politics to Indian feminism, and the ways in which they have responded to them.

Research methods

This book is based on research carried out on the Indian women's movements from 1995 to 2005. During this period, and indeed before it, I have identified myself (and continue to do so) as an Indian feminist, and as a member of feminist organisations in Delhi (Saheli and Gender Studies Group) from 1995–96 and Mumbai (Forum Against Oppression of Women, henceforth FAOW) from 1996 to 2001. In 2001, I relocated to the UK; however continue to be on the mailing list of FAOW. My positionality as a 'fellow feminist' shaped my research, both in influencing the contours of the questions I asked and in giving me privileged access to 'source material' both written and verbal, from within the feminist movements in India. It also gave me a sense of added responsibility – I was faced with the dilemmas of representation and fears of violating trust. Therefore my research methodology can be described as partially using the 'participant observation' method, which involves participating in the lives and cultures of the people who are being studied, in order to get an 'insider's' perspective; while observing them in objective terms (Cox 2004, 3). However as I already considered myself an 'insider' within the Indian feminist movements – as I still do – the degree of 'objectivity' in the observation of Indian feminists may be somewhat inconsistent.

In addition to 'observing' feminists, my research involved collecting and exploring as source material formal interviews with women's movement activists, and papers, pamphlets and statements by women's groups. Therefore I have analysed papers and documentation available in various feminist documentation centres and agencies, including Jagori and Saheli in Delhi; FAOW, Women's Research and Action Group, Akhshara, Majlis Manch and Women's Centre, Mumbai. In addition, 15 semi structured interviews with activists and members from different agencies, including Special Cell to Help Women and Children; FAOW; Akshara; Bhartiya Mahila Federation; the Mumbai Police; CITU and Blue Star Trade Unions; Communist Party of India (henceforth CPI); Communist Party of India Marxist (henceforth CPIM); Akshara; Annapurna Mahila Mandal and Stree Jagruti Samiti informed the research; as did numerous informal but enriching discussions with colleagues from FAOW, Saheli and Akshara. The semi-structured interviews were conducted by prior arrangement, and questions were asked about the organisational structure, views on Indian feminism and where they located themselves in connection with feminist politics, views on legal feminist reform, and their own experiences within varied campaigns. The 'informal' discussions with feminist colleagues and friends often took more varied directions.

In addition, I have critically examined legislative debates from the Lok Sabha from the late 1970s; to access the nature of legislative debates on issues ranging from the marriage laws; rape; dowry; domestic violence; prostitution and civil and personal rights of Muslim women. I have also analysed over 35 case law judgements on domestic violence; rape, personal law; sexual harassment and prostitution. Both these sources bring out diverse, often contradictory trends within official discourse, sometimes displaying direct, sometimes oblique perceptions of feminist ideologies and interventions, which is at times integrated, at others negated or undermined. In my opinion, a close study of legislative debates is important for various reasons. One, because there is an effort to co-opt feminist claims to the benefit of the State, and a recognition of the strength of feminist activism at that point of time. Legislative debates reveal that the interests of the State cannot always be collated with the interests of the one or the other political party, even as the ruling party tries to integrate, most often unsuccessfully, the varied interests of different political parties and lobbies.

Relationship between 'western' and 'Indian' feminisms

The relationship between 'western' and 'Indian' feminisms has been one of intense debates within the Indian women's movement; Indian feminists simultaneously claiming an international feminist solidarity with groups and individuals worldwide, including the west and a specific 'Indian' sensitivity. In the 1970s, the rise of liberal and radical feminism in the west meant that the focus of the international decade of women (1975–1985) was around demands for equal opportunities in education and employment and focus on ending violence against women. In India, the newly emerging feminist movement based its appeal to these varied values and concepts, while examining the ways in which women in India had not benefited from international 'development'. Therefore the 'Status of Women' report commissioned by the State focused both on 'liberal' issues of women's education and employment and on 'radical' ones of violence (Guha et. al. 1976), revealing that Indian feminists in this period were both influenced by western debates, but were able to adapt the debates creatively due to national and local concerns.

Indian feminists have often made demands to the Indian State for amendments in law and policy based on international developments; most often the appeal is based on the Indian State's acceptance of international conventions. Therefore feminist demands to legislate against specific forms of what are considered gender-based violence, including trafficking into prostitution and sexual harassment in the workplace are legitimised in part by appeals to conventions such as the Convention Against Discrimination of Women (CEDAW) and the Convention on Combating the Crimes of Trafficking in Women and Children (Gangoli 2000). In the case of other issues such as dowry related violence against women, Sati, sex selective abortions and custodial rape, in the main feminists focused on the specific manifestations of indigenous patriarchies that were seen as being reflected within these forms of gender-based violence (Kumari 1989; Kishwar and Vanita 1994). However, in such cases appeals can be made on the basis of the need to modernise according to western standards of gender equality; and in others feminists have suggested that some of these forms of violence against women are less specifically 'Indian' than reflecting a wider global trend of patriarchal oppression of women (Rudd 2001; Talwar Oldenburg 2002).

While influences from the west have been acknowledged by several feminist activists, and theorists (see for instance: Gandhi and Shah 1989; Chaudhuri 2004); there are several indications within women's movement activism that it is not a case of 'borrowing' outside context. The campaigns against violence against women included an in-depth and sophisticated understanding of the nature of Indian society. Therefore, as we will see in Chapter 5, the anti-rape campaign in the 1980s and 1990s exposed the nature of the 'third world' system of governance, felt first during the Emergency years through the sterilisation campaigns, and suspension of fundamental rights. The anti-rape campaign focused initially on the police as the visible representatives of State power and brutality against women. Therefore, unlike the anti-rape campaigns in the west in the period, where the focus was more on the interpersonal nature of sexual assault, including within the family and within relationships (Lees 1996), the Indian campaign focused on the systematised structural violence. As I will show in Chapters 4 and 5, organisations such as the Forum Against Rape (henceforth FAR) combined a radical feminist understanding of rape as male violence against women with a 'socialist' conceptualisation of rape as a form of violence against women that had impacts on class and caste relationships within the country. Similarly, the campaigns on domestic violence focused initially, on dowry related murders and the role of mothers-in-law as perpetrators of violence against women. Dowry related violence was understood as a form of gender-based violence that was based on the low status of women in general as disposable. The spread of dowry from an essentially upper caste Brahmin and Hindu custom to a 'nationally' adopted one among varied castes and communities – sometimes replacing the more egalitarian custom of bride price – has also been understood as a form of increased consumerisation of contemporary Indian society, where the traditionally low status of women had led to a further marginalisation of their rights (Gandhi and Shah 1989; Kumari 1989; Judd 2001). While the role and significance of dowry as causing or even reflecting women's unequal status has been disputed (Talwar-Oldenburg 2002),[1] women's organisations in India continue to address the issue of dowry either through its connections to marital violence, or as a reflection of women's unequal status.

Therefore while the Indian women's movement is influenced by, and influences, western debates on feminism, it is unusual within feminisms in the strong links it has forged with other social movements. Therefore unlike in the west, Indian feminists – including those within separatist feminist organisations – work with left-wing movements on issues relating to women's rights. As I will see in the course of this book, the relationship between leftist party women's activists (who often do not identify themselves as feminists) can sometimes be tense, there is on the whole a sense of working together on most issues. In addition, feminists both support other social movements such as environmental and anti globalisation movements (Baviskar 1995), caste struggles and gay rights movements, but also raise the women's issues within these movements.

In spite of the nuances within feminist conceptualisations of Indian society, the rhetoric of 'westernisation' has been used consistently as a charge to embarrass and silence feminists. For instance, feminist opposition to servile portrayals of 'Hindu' women as ideal wives in cinema[2] or opposition to Sati in 1984 (Nandy 1998) or support for cinematic representations of lesbianism (Kapur 2000) have been constructed as the actions of women divorced from quintessential 'Indian' values. A possible rationale for this critique can be seen as the threat posed by feminists to the personal sphere of the home, manifested in feminist critiques of 'traditional' sexual and personal relations based on female subordination. As historians of colonial India

---

1   Talwar-Oldenburg offers a critique of dowry as a form of gender violence, preferring to see it in terms of women's inheritance and status in general terms. For more details, see Chapter 6.

2   See Chapter 4 for more details.

have demonstrated, Indian nationalism in the nineteenth and early twentieth century characterised the home and therefore domestic arrangements as an areas where colonialism could not and indeed should not impact; hence nationalist struggles were fought at the public arena, and to protect the home from the 'colonial encounter' (Mani 1998). The need to protect the home – and by extension, gender relations within the home – from the corrupting influences of the west is a continuing concern in contemporary India, one with which feminists are constantly confronted by.

Debates within feminisms on law

Within feminist activism and discourse in India, debates on the role of law have been central. Feminist interventions and attitudes to law are varied, and multiple, but are united in that they contain an implicit or explicit critique of patriarchy. Areas of concern, as I will show during the course of this book, are an examination of how law constructs and legitimises social hierarchies, and differences between men and women; while sometimes working to transform law according to feminist principles and values. Feminist critique of Indian law has recognised that law and judicial practices legitimise women's subordination. This is understood as being expressed through a range of civil and criminal laws, that work to discriminate against women. Feminists have pointed out that laws relating to marriage, divorce, inheritance, succession, guardianship preserve the family as it exists, that is as 'a system based on male dominance and control of female sexuality and reproduction' (Haksar nd, 2). One could add that the control of women's sexuality is not restricted to the civil laws listed above, but to a range of criminal laws. Besides, the experience of women within the legal system demonstrates that the judiciary and the police often underscore patriarchal values and ideologies.

Debates on law have also politicised, and brought to the forefront, an understanding of violence against women, based on the perception that there is systematic and systematised aggression against women, naturalised through different forms of violence. These include rape, sexual harassment in the workplace and in public places, pornography, trafficking, prostitution, selective sex determination, female infanticide, child marriage, dowry and domestic violence. In other words, a range of events and incidents experienced by women both within the home, and outside; where perpetrators can be male or female family members, members of the wider community or representatives of the State are conceptualised as violence. While some of these meanings are disputed – as we will see in Chapter 3 and Chapter 6; the links between trafficking and dowry is disputed. However, the act of naming these practices as violence against women serves to question the normative nature of such interactions; and is therefore seen as a radical act.

Some feminists have therefore asked for legal reform of law based on feminist understandings of law; therefore influencing legislative debates and contributing to the creation of new laws, or the amendment of old laws, on various aspects of violence against women. Changes in law have been among the tangible 'results' of the campaigns of feminist movements. Therefore, since the early 1980s, amendments have been made to the rape laws (1983); there has been an inclusion of a domestic violence clause in the criminal code (1983); and in 2005, the Domestic Violence Act has been passed that extended the right to matrimonial property to women experiencing domestic violence. The rape of a development worker employed by the state during the course of her work, led to a campaign that has resulted in what is considered a landmark judgement (1997) and a national law (2003) on sexual harassment in the workplace. In addition, the state has responded to demands of women's organisations to stop selective sex pre-selection, by passing a national law banning it in 1993 and to campaigns against media projections of women by passing the Indecent Representation of Women (Prohibition) Act, 1986. Yet, as feminists have recognised, the laws passed have been in the main ineffective and in some cases worked against the interests of women.[3]

However, as we will see throughout this book, while working to change law, sections of the women's movement have expressed a degree of skepticism with law, and legal changes. A question that has been raised is whether law is indeed a 'subversive site' for feminists (Kapur and Cossman 1996), therefore whether working with law allows feminists to challenge patriarchy effectively. It has been suggested therefore, that the experience of the 1980s and the 1990s, where changes in law on rape, domestic violence for example, did not benefit the lives of women, or even encourage a more feminist construction of the category 'woman' in Indian law, raises doubts about the transformative capacity of law. In addition, it has been suggested that that feminist engagements with law and rights within law can 'radically refract the ethical and emancipatory impulse of feminism itself' (Menon 1995b, 369). It is suggested that the language of rights can be alienating and individualistic, that the discourse on rights like that of justice is restrictive and counter productive for feminism, as the latter aims at homogenising meaning (Menon 2004). Laws are seen as 'categorising, concretising, and regulating (sexual or otherwise) behavior, which can be inimical to the interests of marginal groups' (Menon 1995b, 370; Menon 2004).

While these criticisms have been the focus of debate within Indian feminism, at a general level, it is safe to postulate that most feminists have little or no faith in legal solutions to violence. These include both 'academic' feminists like Menon (2004) but to some extent activists and feminists lawyers who both work with the law as a way of providing relief to women, while accepting its limitations (Gandhi and Shah 1989; Agnes 1992; Agnes 1995) as they feel that there may not be viable alternatives other than the formal structure of law. Therefore, for many feminists law remains a significant arena for feminist intervention, and the dreams of a feminist jurisprudence are not completely abandoned.

---

3   For instance, The Indecent Representation of Women (Prohibition) Act, 1986 is not only ineffective in curbing such representations, it also enables the State to increase its own power. For more details, see Chapter 6..

Challenges: Caste, community and globalisation

Caste, class and community stratification in contemporary India are significant areas of concern for feminist activism. As in the case of gender, the Indian constitution provides guarantees that seek to balance the rights of religious minorities and historically marginalised caste groups. These include Article 14 that guarantee right to equal protection under the law; Article 15 that forbids discrimination on the basis of religion, race, caste, sex, place of birth; Article 25 which guarantees freedom of religion and Article 29 that guarantees to minorities the right to conserve their culture.

Caste

Only Hindus have traditionally followed the caste system, though it has affected the social stratification within Muslim and Christian communities. Within the traditional caste hierarchy, there are four Varnas or castes. Brahmins are predominantly the ideologically dominant caste controlling ritual and scholarly pursuits; Kshatriyas are the warrior caste; Vaishyas are the trading caste and Sudras are agricultural or labouring castes. A fifth Varna emerged, that were seen as Achyut or untouchable castes. These were treated as polluting castes; and these castes have in post independent India renamed themselves Dalit, which relates to the oppression suffered to them; rather than the ascribed pollution. In addition, there are tribes in different parts of the country are considered to be 'outside' the caste system. Caste hierarchies in contemporary India are fluid, and as we have seen, caste based discrimination has been prohibited in the Indian constitution, and there are provisions for positive discrimination in education and employment. However, there is evidence that Dalits and tribals continue to suffer structural inequalities and sustained poverty (Fuller 1997), and experience organised periodic violence from 'upper castes' in some parts of the country.

There has been some criticism from Dalit groups that Indian feminism represents and is made up of upper caste and upper class Hindu women (Chudhuri 2004). Representatives of Dalit women's organisations have suggested that within Indian feminist movements, Dalit women are projected as 'having only experience, not intelligence' (Manorama 2006), therefore alluding to the ways in which the interests of Dalit women have been marginalised within Indian women's movements. It has also been argued that communist parties in West Bengal have subscribed to upper caste notions of gender relations, ignoring and marginalising lower caste women's perceptions (Ray and Korteweg 1999, 61). Debates on caste and gender oppression have also been raised in the context of debates on reservations of seats for women in parliament and state assemblies in 2000, where it has been argued by OBC (Other Backward Caste) members of different political parties that there should be a 'sub-reservation' for women from these castes, on the basis that caste fractures gender identity, and 'lower caste' women's interests are best represented by women from these castes, which has been opposed by some feminists (Sen 2000, 53–4).

Women from within Dalit castes have formed organisations such as the All India Dalit Women's Forum in 1994 and the National Federation of Dalit Women and Dalit Solidarity in 1995, and various regional dalit women's groups link caste relations to gender exploitation, and have focused on sexual violence, therefore suggesting that rape, the stripping and parading of women, and other gendered forms of humiliation lead to the perpetuation of upper caste dominance, as does the 'hyper-exploitation of dalit women's labour' (Rao 2003) perpetuate dominance by upper-caste men. In addition, Dalit women's organisation focus on the gendered implications of other caste based violence and oppression, such as the demolition of Dalit dominated urban slums in various cities in India, and the ways in which Dalit women suffer the consequences of urban poverty and displacement (Manorama 2006).

While the upper caste composition of sections of the Indian feminist movements cannot be denied, it is however important to note that caste analysis has played in some feminist visions of justice, and in the varied composition of the movement. As we will see during the course of this book, campaigns against custodial rape (Chapter 5) have challenged the structural inequalities that Dalit and tribal women face, and feminist analyses of the Hindu civil laws on marriage, divorce, inheritance, maintenance and guardianship have included a sharp critique of the Brahmanical underpinnings of existing laws that work against women's interests (Chapter 3).

Hindu fundamentalism and minority feminisms

The rise of Hindu fundamentalism in post colonial India has been analysed as having its origins in the 'divide and rule' policy successfully implemented under colonial rule, contributing to partition of India and Pakistan in 1947, that accompanied independence from colonial rule (see for instance: Sarkar 1985; Butalia 2000; Kakar 1995). Prior to independence, Hindu fundamentalism was represented by the Rashtriya Seva Sangh (henceforth RSS) founded in 1925, and the RSS continues to see itself as 'the antidote to…the dangerous tendencies of modern-day tendencies' (Narula 2003, 44) including secularism. Post independence, India adopted a secular constitution, but the newly created Indian State simultaneously witnessed communal riots, that took the form of widespread carnage against Muslims; leading to loss of life, and a sense of insecurity for the Muslim community. The post colonial state saw the emergence and electoral success of Hindu fundamentalist political parties, both nationally represented by the Bhartiya Janata Party (henceforth BJP) and regionally, represented by the Shiv Sena in Maharashtra. Feminists have argued that religious fundamentalism in India reflects the crisis of both modernisation and of democracy, and has serious implications for women's rights, and women's movements, arguing that 'fundamentalism…refashions patriarchies to legitimise participation of women in the nationalist project' (FAOW 2005, 3). Fundamentalist projects therefore underscore patriarchy by projecting and promoting 'traditional' views of women as mothers and wives, and controlling women's appearance through impositions of dress codes. Women's bodies, as we will see, are seen symbolically to represent community and family honour (FAOW 2005).

In the partition riots, women from different religious communities including Muslim women were targeted through sexual assault, with the bodies of women being constructed as a repository of the honour of the community (Menon 1998; Butalia 2000). This is a recurrent theme in subsequent communal riots, including the 2002 Gujarat riots, where Muslim women's bodies were specifically targeted sexually during communal riots by Hindu fundamentalist forces. In addition minority communities especially Muslims (and to a less degree Christians) have experienced structural discrimination, leading to Muslim communities being economically, educationally and socially marginalised (International Initiative for Justice in Gujarat 2003) which have specific implications for women.

As we will see throughout the book, Indian feminists have been cognizant of, and responsive to challenges from communalisation of Indian society. In addition to working closely in periods of communal unrest with other secular forces (International Initiative for Justice in Gujarat 2003), feminists have responded to the specific implications of communalisation for women. As we will see in Chapter 3, there has been a rethinking of the feminist demand for a gender just civil code, due to a cooption of feminist arguments by rightwing forces, leading to a shift to alternative solutions, including internal community reforms. In addition, as with Dalit feminism, minority women in the Indian women's movement have claimed that they have felt isolated and alienated within the movement, because of the predominantly Hindu symbols used within the movement, including Hindu goddesses such as Kali and Shakti being used as metaphors for the strengths of Indian women (Dietrich 1992, 11),[4] therefore collapsing 'Hindu' with 'Indian'. It has also been suggested by some minority women that the logic of 'internal reforms' adopted by sections of the feminist movements leads to increased responsibility for minority women within the movement, as minority laws are projected as inherently more backward and anti women, though changes are as much needed in Hindu law, and the Special Marriages Act (henceforth SMA). Communalisation has also impacted access to criminal law for women. As we will see in Chapter 6, communal riots against Muslims in 1992–93 in Mumbai, and in Gujarat in 2002 and the complicity of the police and civil administration in the anti Muslim violence led to a decline in faith in the 'rule of law' for Muslim communities (Centre for Society and Secularism 1994). During and following communal riots, Muslim women find themselves with less access to community or civil society support, whether in the case of sexual assault by members of the majority community, or domestic violence by their own family members. In particular, Muslim women find it difficult to approach the police for cases of domestic violence.

Globalisation

India experienced a transition to globalisation, initiated through what has been called 'market reforms' in 1991. These changes include: increased reliance on the market

---

4   See Chapter 3 for more details.

mechanism manifested through state policies including deregulation of the Indian economy, reduction of governmental controls, increased autonomy for private investment, reduced state investment in the public sector, foreign capital given greater access to the Indian market (Sen 1996), and have led to intense debates on whether these 'reforms' have improved the lives of women and men in the country. On the one hand it has been suggested that these changes have rewarded India with a more efficient system of economic governance, with decreased governmental control and regulation, on the other critics have suggested the main beneficiaries of liberalization of the economy have been the middle classes, and that the process of globalisation has increased social and economic stratification in contemporary India (Sen 1996, 9). Left-wing parties in India, who see in deregulation an erosion of labour rights for the urban working class, and decline in agricultural profits for the rural poor, have opposed globalisation; as have environmental movements such as the Narmada Bachao Andolan, who analyse 'development' as contributing to increased marginalisation of tribal communities. It has been argued that loss of resources has serious repercussions for working class and tribal women, as liberalisation has been analysed as leading to a loss of livelihood and traditional resource bases, forced displacement and increased impoverishment (Baviskar 1995).

The impact of globalisation on women has been the focus of feminist debate, with some arguing that these economic changes have led to increased hardships for working class and lower caste women, both economically and socially. Feminists have noted the ways in which multi-national companies in India, as in other parts of the world exploit the labour of 'young, underpaid and disadvantaged women' in free trade zones and sweat shops; and call centres use 'young lower middle class, educated women' (FAOW 2005, 2) with few effective labour rights, or limited rights for collective action.

In addition, multinational corporations attempt to homogenise a universal image of the body of the ideal women through advertisements, leading to increased commodification of women's bodies (Eisenstein 2004; FAOW 2005, 2). This is manifested, as we will see in Chapter 3, in nationalist pride vested in the bodies of Indian women winning international beauty pageants. While some feminists feel that these developments have led to women enjoying greater sexual autonomy, and increased control over their own bodies (Ghosh 1996), others fear that these developments are reflections of consumerism, and contribute to increased commodification of the female body that serves male fantasies (Kishwar 1996). Similarly in Chapter 4 it will be seen how debates on representation of women's bodies are divided on an understanding of whether the global influences of satellite TV in the 1990s have contributed to women's liberation, or its reverse, enslavement by consumerist ethos and increased commodification of women's bodies.

As we have already seen in the introductory chapter, Indian feminism is characterised above all, by its passionate allegiance to polyvocality, and respect for difference and differences. The concerns that I have touched upon in the introduction – the influence of western and global feminisms experienced as positive by some feminists and rejected by others; debates around the role of law in feminist debates, and challenges faced by caste oppression, communal differences and the influence of global capital – will be examined throughout the book. This book will hopefully bring out some of the many ways in which Indian feminist movement have tackled these challenges.

Chapter 2

National and Local Feminisms: Different Streams within the Women's Movements

This chapter will offer a brief historical survey of feminism nationally and in the city Bombay from the nineteenth century to the early twenty-first century, focusing more on feminisms since the 1970s. While women's organisations and what has been called the 'woman question' has been a part of anti-colonial nationalist movements in the late nineteenth and early twentieth century (Sarkar 1989), it was only in the 1970s that feminist groups that worked essentially for women's interests were formed. Indian feminists have recognised and acknowledged differences between themselves. What they share is recognition of differential power relations between women and men, with men enjoying power over women. The recognition, does not, as we will see, detract from the recognition that not all men are equal in relation to each other, indeed that not all women are similarly placed in positions of subordination.

Nationally, the emergence of feminism in the 1970s has been attributed to an expansion of educational and employment opportunities for women, disillusionment with existing political structures owing to the perceived excesses of the Emergency, and a feeling of disillusionment with mainstream left-wing parties, which seemed to accord a low priority to what were called 'women's issues'. This was also the period when several 'people's movements' were at their peak, feeding in to an exciting sense of political upheaval. Some of these were: the Naxalite movements in West Bengal, Bihar and Andhra Pradesh, the anti-price movements in Maharashtra and students movements in different parts of the country (Gandhi 1996).

Within Bombay, the context of the late 1970s and early 1980s complemented this trend. However, within the powerful trade union and left-wing parties so active in the city at that point, some women found themselves alienated and marginalised when they raised issues of women's oppression. In this chapter, I will try to explore some of these factors – intertwining the national and the local – to trace the growth of feminist movements in Bombay. I will also focus on some prominent feminist groups, such as: FAOW, Mumbai (an autonomous feminist collective), Stree Jagruti Samiti (a nation-wide CPI (ML) party-based organisation), Awaaz-e-Niswaan and Annapurna Mahila Mandal, Mumbai (an employment service based organisation). I will examine the organisational structures, ideologies and working strategies of these organisations.

Internationally, women's issues gained prominence with the declaration of the decade 1975–1985 as the international decade for Women. In India, the state responded by commissioning a report on the status of women to a group of feminist researchers and activists, which acknowledged that women in India suffered from a range of structural inequalities and injustices (Guha et. al. 1974). Indian feminists in this period were influenced by western debates on violence against women, based on consciousness raising groups in the 1970s and leading to refuge provision for women experiencing domestic violence (Hague et. al. 2003). However the different historical and social trajectory of Indian women meant that these debates had to be adapted creatively, or some aspects of them had to be rejected.

As noted the sense of alienation experienced by some women in leftist movements in Bombay in the 1970s and 1980s became an impetus for separatist feminist activism. However within the nascent feminist groups, there was also an acceptance of the validity of social movements working against poverty, corruption, caste and class. Feminist movements in India have since their growth in the 1970s, acknowledged the need for links with such social movements, therefore unlike in the west, ideas of a feminist separatist state (Mackinnon 1989) were never taken seriously, or addressed.

The background

Women's mobilisation, colonialism and national movements

In the early nineteenth century, what has been called the 'woman question' was raised primarily by elite upper caste Hindu men. The 'woman question' included issues such as women's education, widow remarriage and campaigns against Sati (Sarkar 1989). In addition, some upper caste Hindu women rejected the constraints that they faced within Brahminical traditions (Chakravari 1998). As historians have pointed out, social reform that focussed on improving women's 'status' was somewhat weakened in the late nineteenth century, due to emerging nationalist movements in India that resisted 'colonial interventions in gender relations' (Sen 2000, 10) especially in the areas of family relations. Therefore campaigns such as those against Sati and widow remarriage that had been supported by social reformist colonial representatives were seen as 'internal' matters to be decided within the community. In the mid- to late nineteenth-century, there was therefore nationalist resistance to colonial attempts at 'modernisation' of the Hindu family, as in the Age of Consent controversy that resulted from the government's attempt to raise the marriage age for women. Sen argues that the liberal and 'civilising' arm of the colonial state was 'disabled by indigenous opposition' (Sen 2000, 11) that led to the entrenchment of upper caste patriarchal norms within legal structures. As we will see in Chapter 3, some of these debates – especially the right of the State to intervene in the private – are still raised in the context of contemporary Indian politics, and different religious communities continue to resist the intervention of the Indian State into the 'private' sphere of marriage, the family and gender relations.

In the 1920s Indian women entered into a new era – with what is defined as 'feminism' (Sen 2000, 14) leading to the creation of localised women's associations that worked on issues of women's education, livelihood strategies for working class women, as well as national level women's associations such as the All India Women's Conference. The latter were closely allied to the Indian National Congress, and worked within the nationalist and anti-colonial movements, and under Mahatma Gandhi's leadership, mass mobilisation of women became an integral part of nationalism. Women therefore played an important role in various nationalist and anti-colonial struggles including the civil disobedience movements in the 1930s (Sarkar 1985).

During this period, sections of the organised left created their own women's organisations such as the Mahila Atmaraksha Samiti, but these worked on general, rather than gendered issues, and this period saw the beginning of the subordination of women's issues to mass and working class issues (Sen 2000, 15–22).

While women's organisations such as the All India Women's Conference continued to operate in the years following independence, and the Communist Party of India created its women's wing (National Federation of Indian Women) in 1954, feminist movements were less active immediately after independence in 1947, with nationalist agendas on nation building taking precedence over feminist concerns.

The early 1970s and the National Emergency

The early 1970s were militant and active years for Marxist–Leninist politics and other popular movements in various parts of India. One such movement, as documented by Nandita Gandhi's pioneering study was the anti-price rise movement (henceforth APRM) in Maharashtra in the early 1980s (Gandhi 1996).

Anti-price Rise Movement

This movement struck a chord in the hearts and minds of working and middle class women in a way that leftist and working class politics had not succeeded or even tried to do. The APRM died out in a few years – it could not survive the repression unleashed by the State during the Emergency. However during its short tenure, it articulated the anger and the resentment of the common people regarding the unprecedented price rise of essential commodities like wheat, rice, sugar, oil and other foodstuffs. These items became dearer by about 25 per cent in the course of a few months.

The leaders of the APRM were women active in the national and local left-wing movements, many of whom were married to men active in the trade union movement. Some of the women were members of the women's wing of left-wing political parties, such as National Federation of Indian Women (NFIW) and Janwadi Mahila Samiti (Democratic Women's Organisation, henceforth JMS). These women, while politically active, were confronted with the responsibility of looking after their families. As one of the participants pointed out:

> The children (of couples like us) were mostly looked after by mothers, aunts or servants. It was not expected of the fathers to share the responsibilities. Anyhow, how could they? It was impossible because of the crazy hours they kept (quoted in Gandhi 1996, 51).

Gandhi points out that while most of these women had defied their natal homes by objecting to traditional practices, such as arranged marriages, few questioned the institution of marriage or the sexual division of labour within the family. This was reflected in the rhetoric of the movement, as women were mobilised to protest in their capacity as wives and mothers, not as citizens of a country against an unjust economic policy. Women were entreated to fight as an extension of their housewifely duties. The appeal may have effective as a mobilising strategy, but it narrowed the political strength of the movement.

The leaders of the movement rejected what they projected as separatist feminist politics, as this extract from a NFIW booklet published in 1974 reveals. The 'women's angle' was recognised as being different from 'general' issues, but it was suggested that it could not be fought for on its own, and that general progress of the country would benefit women as well as men.

> We have to struggle by the side of the exploited people with our men folk to build common actions which could change society into an egalitarian one. No doubt, women's organisations...will stress on the problem from the women's angle... but the efforts should be to support all general issues that advance the welfare of the nation and therefore, of half the population – the women (Quoted in Gandhi 1996, 115).

In spite of some discomfort with what was euphemistically called the 'women's angle', the APRM did have a strong connection with women's politics. This was recognised by the leaders themselves who called it the 'new women's movement.' Gandhi holds that the APRM holds a vital place of its own in history, standing as it does, between two phases of the women's movement – the women's movement attached to the nationalist movement in late nineteenth-century and early twentieth-century and the feminist movements emerging from the late 1970s (Gandhi 1996, 1–3).

Some strategies that were adopted were raids on traders, inspection of ration shops, and release of commodities from government and market stocks by women. Mrinal Gore organised a *gherao* (demonstration) in Aarey Milk colony to protest against inferior milk sold at inflated rates. In 1973, a *Latni Morcha,* literally, rolling pin demonstration, was organised in which 10,000 women participated and demonstrated on the streets on Bombay with their rolling pins (Gandhi, 1996), therefore symbolically challenging the image of the housewife as docile and controllable, using the *latni* as a powerful symbol of militant action.

Powerful as this movement was, it collapsed when the Emergency was announced. One can speculate that at least two reasons can be put forward for this. One, that since this was constructed as a 'women's issue', it was accorded less priority by the leaders than other political issues, therefore at the time of a national crisis, it was withdrawn to fight other battles. Secondly, the nature of the movement could not survive the sustained control unleashed on people's movements during the Emergency.

The National Emergency

The declaration of the Emergency came as a shock to many quarters in 1975. The Indian state did not appear to be suffering from any crisis or threat, which merited such an extreme step, even though that was the 'official' rationale put forward by the ruling Prime Minister, Indira Gandhi. The following extract is from a speech made by her while proclaiming the Emergency:

> I am sure you are all conscious of the deep and widespread conspiracy, which has been brewing...the forces of disintegration are in full play and communal passions are being aroused, threatening our unity...the new emergency proclamations will in no way affect the rights of law abiding citizens (Government of India 1984, 177–178).

In spite of this assurance, the Emergency meant a suspension of civil liberties and rights. Political thinkers have challenged the official defence of the Emergency, suggesting that the factors leading to the Emergency was not a united nationwide challenge to the Indian State, but public discontent against the government led by Indira Gandhi (Babu 1995). It was therefore Mrs Gandhi's inability to distinguish between her personal interests, and those of the nation that led to the draconian measures during the Emergency, which affected various people's movements, including Naxalite movements, the APRM and Jayaprakash Narayan's movement through the arrests of political activists. This was combined with censorship of the print media and television that made it almost impossible for conflicting views to be expressed in these foray. The overwhelming memories of those days are those of a general feeling of terror, created to paralyse dissent:

> Fear, born of dissent, was more acute – particularly among the innocent – during the Emergency than it was during the two centuries of British rule. More than 150,000 people were detained for an indefinite period without trial. There were prominent figures like Jayaprakash Narayan, as well as the humble and nameless who will never figure on the roll-call of honour, who withstood the hundred thousand petty tyrants who mushroomed all over the country during the Emergency (Palkhiwala 1995).

In some ways, the Emergency initiated a new political order in India. Salman Rushdie, in an incisive essay, written in 1985, compared the Emergency to the opening of Pandora's box, suggesting that the Emergency represented 'the triumph of cynicism in Indian public life' and that most of the evils besetting contemporary India, including corruption, lack of respect for the democratic process and the electorate and the 'resurgence of religious extremism' could be traced back to the Emergency (Rushdie 1991, 52).

The shock of being confronted with a state which has been seen so far as benign, at least by the self-consciously apolitical middle class, 'turning' autocratic and oppressive was worsened by what was seen as an attack on the personal life and liberty of Indian citizens, manifested in the policy of forcible sterilisation carried out on men as a part of the family planning programme. A study published in 1978 under the auspices of the Centre for Policy Research and the Family Planning Foundation found that there was a generalised, and intense fear of the Government, particularly with regard to family planning. They discovered that most of the 'acceptors' of the programme were in reality, unwilling participants, who had been brought forcibly to the camps. Sterilisation had been performed on men who 'looked too old and long past their youth to need it' and on unmarried and childless young men (Pai Panandikar et. al. 1978, 108–113; also see Lok Sabha Debates 1976, 155 and 198). While the programme was carried out at a national level, its effects were felt most strongly by the poor, as it was believed that the 'problem' of over-population was due to the large number of children produced by the poor (Lok Sabha Debates 1976, 144 and 183). Both men and women opposed the male sterilisation programme, as women considered male vasectomy as a 'direct assault on the sanctity of the family life, on the supreme status accorded to the husbands and on the very institution of marriage' (Panicker 1995).

While the hostility against the state generated among women was no doubt partly due to conventional reasons – the feeling that the 'superiority' of the husband was being threatened, there was nevertheless an element of confrontation with the state. At a general level, the hostility of the people was expressed at a national level by the defeat suffered by Indira Gandhi in the general elections of 1977.[1] It has been suggested that that the impact of the Emergency was not a wholly negative one, as it led to the establishing of dissent, resistance and protest, leading to a situation where 'some of the most excluded and oppressed among the masses have been acquiring a sense of individual and collective potency' (Kothari 1995), therefore leading to the creation of civil liberties and democratic rights groups. However, most of these civil rights and democratic rights groups could not completely fulfil the aspirations of women in the political context of the 1970s, therefore leading to the emergence of groups of women who were autonomous of the human rights groups, as of left-wing parties.[2]

---

1   The failure of the family planning programme during the Emergency, which focused mostly on male sterilisation had another effect on the family planning programme in later years. The focus shifted from men to women and the nature of coercion changed. For more details, see Gangoli (1998).

2   Democratic and civil rights groups did address some issues relating to women's rights in the late 1980s and early 1990s, owing perhaps to the influence of the feminist movements. For instance, the human rights group, the People's Union for Democratic Rights (PUDR) not only takes on significantly identifiable feminist issues, its members, male and female, in the main identify themselves as feminists. See PUDR (1989) and PUDR (1989).

Rise of feminist groups

The nascent feminist groups that emerged in the late 1970s and early 1980s focused essentially around the issues of police and state initiated violence against women. This is hardly surprising given the context of the Emergency and the memories of repression. As we will see in Chapter 4, the first major campaign of the women's movement was around the gang rape of a tribal girl, Mathura by a group of policemen in a police station and the role and complicity of the judiciary in condoning it. Feminists have recognised the impact of the Emergency in the choice of issue, leading to disillusionment with the State, and recognition of the 'oppressive machinery of the state in action' (Vibhuti et. al. 1983, 182). Therefore, the campaign focused on the nature of third world States, which the Emergency years had exposed as repressive and opaque. The police and the police station represented the visible powers of the state; indeed the police had played a central role in unleashing repression and torture during this period. All these contradictions seem to come together in the Mathura campaign, later extended to include other cases of custodial rape.

The anti-rape campaign took off in different cities of the country almost simultaneously. In Mumbai, FAR was formed on 12 January 1980, made up of a conglomerate of women, some already active in left-wing parties, others who had entered politics for the first time. In other parts of India, autonomous women's group emerged, including Saheli and Stree Sangharsh in Delhi, Asmita in Hyderabad and Vimochana in Bangalore. While I will be looking at the anti-rape campaign else where in the book (See Chapter 4 and 5), here we can note two aspects that are related to this chapter. First, that while protests had been made against the use of rape as a weapon to suppress democratic movements, it was only in this period that this issue was articulated not merely as a civil rights issue, but as a women's issue, and an issue of violence against women. Secondly, the anti-rape campaign, and the domestic violence campaign in the 1980s mark the differences in issues raised by the Indian Women's Movement, and feminists in the west. While the broad issue was the same – violence against women – the specific instances of violence taken up remained uniquely Indian. In the case of rape, unlike in the west, marital rape was not the major plank of intervention (Lees 1996). The focus was on sexual violence by the police on the most marginalised of Indian society, i.e., poor, lower caste or minority women. In the case of marital violence, the Indian feminists focused primarily on dowry related violence and murders, which was again a part of Indian cultural context.

As we have seen before, some women entered the political arena for the first time with the anti-rape campaign, while others had been, and continue to be, an active part of the left-wing and trade union movements. It is the latter that I propose to examine in the next section.

Trade union struggles and feminism

The history of twentieth-century Mumbai is one of militant trade union struggles, due to the centrality of the cotton mill industry to the social and economic structure of the city until the early 1990s. Women workers have played a prominent role in several work related struggles and have benefited from union activities (Rohini PH et.al nd, 131; Gangoli 1993). However, women workers and issues around women's rights are often seen as less important than 'general' issues of wages and working conditions. Trade unions have consistently held that concentrating on women's issues divides the working class and since there are fewer women workers than male workers, their issues and concerns are those of a minority and do not provide a basis for class struggle (Krishnaraj 1986, 9–10), therefore most trade unions do not address issues of structural inequality against women that lead to discrimination against them in the workplace, including differential wages for male and female workers or sexual harassment in the workplace. A communist trade unionist active in the textile industry for over 35 years admitted that he could not recall a single agitation that has frontally taken up any issue pertaining to women, such as maternity benefits, equal pay for equal pay.[3] Unions often construct the worker as male, and articulate their struggles within the context of preserving the family structure, and protecting male workers within the family. Women working within trade unions often take up a consciously anti-feminist stance:

> We are not a feminist organisation, we are not anti-men. We are not the only ones who are exploited, Harijan men are no less exploited...One has to be a good, sympathetic husband to allow (his) woman to join the struggle (quoted in Jayawardhane and Kelkar 1995, 2123–6).

Issues of domestic violence and sexual abuse are rarely tackled within unions. On the contrary, trade unions have used sexual abuse to silence and disempower women, especially those belonging to rival unions (Gangoli 1993, 22). Domestic violence perpetuated by male union leaders and members on their wives and daughters are not addressed. Where women union members are subjected to such violence, they are often denied a space to articulate their anguish, and indeed most working class women accept domestic violence as a reality of marital life (Purao amd Savara 1983, 12–18). Therefore, unions seem to have failed to create an ambiance in which gendered oppression against its members is taken up. Trade unions believe that patriarchal control can be challenged through struggles that are distinct from, though supported by, and supporting, working class struggles. A CPI activist implied as much:

> Women's organisations have an erroneous impression about trade unions. Trade unions have a limited role, which is to fight economic battles in the workplace. Unless unions fulfil their economic role, workers go away.[4]

While some women working within trade unions expressed discomfort with the nature of gendered inequities within working class politics, there was a sense of despair in being able to address these issues within trade unions:

---

3   Interview with Kadav. CITU activist on 5 February 1992.
4   Malini Tumkule, CPI activist, interviewed on 15 October 1991.

And it was somehow more easy, more natural for male activists to organise r
more difficult and more unnatural for female activists...Gradually, the...pr
to establish themselves. Every one should have equal rights, but there was s
an examination of the 'natural basis' of inequality, there was a theoretical blinu ᵕᵖ
women's rights remained at a mere moral level ... (Leela Bhonsale, quoted in Gail Omvedt
1980, 49).

Within trade union rhetoric, 'working on women's issues' can be seen as creating
schisms within working class families (Gupta 1991,33). A document authored by
the CPI(ML) ends on a prescriptive note to feminists, warning them not to divide
working class families, and suggest that '... any women's movement pitted against
the oppression of the family on women must first learn to fight against the property
relations in that society' (Bhrame et. al 1987, 4). The document argues that feminist
movements sees men as the enemy and equates class oppression with gender
oppression, while in reality the two are distinct, and need to be resolved differently
from class struggle, suggesting that 'contradictions' between the sexes can be resolved
by 'discussion, persuasion and collective assertion', not combatively, unlike class
struggle between the working class and the ruling class (Bhrame et. al 1987, 4).

Feminist responses to these sectarian and often unsympathetic attitudes in the
1980s have been to create spaces for autonomous action, independent of left-wing
and political party affiliations, leading to the emergence of the Autonomous Women's
Movement (AWM). Some feminists have been a part of the left and indeed continue
to identify themselves ideologically with left politics, however have moved away
from the organised left, creating, initiating and participating in feminist collectives.
Others continue to work within left-wing groups and trade unions, rejecting the
AWM as being too closely aligned to western, separatist politics. The next section
will examine some of the groups set up in the 1970s and 1980s in Bombay, the
factors influencing their politics and their choices.

Emergence of feminist groups

From Forum Against Rape to Forum Against Oppression of Women

In the 1980s and 1990s, a number of groups emerged in Bombay and all over
the country, which took up women's issues. These organisations varied in their
perspectives and strategies, but shared a set of assumptions, that was based on an
understanding of women's oppression:

> All women and women's organisations which consider themselves a part of the Indian
> Women's Movement have as their starting premise the belief that women are an oppressed
> section of society, though they may differ in their understanding of class and gender, the
> origins of women's oppression and its perpetuation (Gandhi and Shah 1989, 24).

As we have seen earlier in this chapter, in early 1980s, a group of women came
together to take up the issue of custodial rape in Bombay, which was linked to a

countrywide campaign against rape. Members of FAR identified themselves as an ad hoc body, predominantly made up of westernised women with 'cosmopolitan' values, and well informed about western liberation movements (Vibhuti et. al. 1983, 184). As an issue based federation, FAR lasted only 2 years, and moved on to a forum that addressed broader issues of women's oppression, renaming themselves as Forum Against Oppression of Women in 1982 (FAOW 1990, 2). The broader issues that were addressed – and indeed continue to be addressed – include sexual harassment in the workplace and in public spaces, dowry related violence and murders, domestic violence, representation of women in the media, discrimination against women in civil and criminal law, rights of working class women, including sex workers, women's health and reproductive rights, and support the work of social movements working against poverty, class and caste oppressions.

Advocacy to support: Women's Centre

Working on violence against women created an awareness of the vulnerability of women within the home and outside it, therefore some activists within FAOW felt the need to provide women with support during moments of crisis. This need was partially met in 1981 by the establishment of a feminist group, which called itself Women's Centre. The Centre saw itself as a 'supra-community' for women outside of an oppressive, patriarchal world,[5] working since its inception primarily against domestic violence, even while there was recognition that the workers would not be 'experts' in the areas of counselling or social work. The members of the Centre drew their legitimacy from their identity as feminists, and as women:

> None of us involved in the Centre had a background of professional social work or counselling, but were activists from the women's movement. Few had experienced violence in our own lives and wanted to share the experience with the other women who were in similar situations (FAOW 1990, 4).

The Centre located itself in a middle class locality in the eastern suburbs of the city. The members of the group decided not to work within a working class area in the city, even though their focus was on poor and working class women as they felt that placing themselves within a working class community could be conceived as a challenge to the patriarchies present within such a space. On the other hand, if an alternative space was provided for women that were geographically located at a distance away from their own context, it could provide anonymity to women using it.

The Women's Centre has used non-legal and legal methods of resolving domestic violence. Non-legal methods include public demonstrations outside the home of domestic violence perpetrators, therefore shaming perpetrators and creating social pressure on the families. Women approaching the Centre are supported, whether or not they choose to go down the legal route, and the normative nature of marriage

---

5   Based on verbal presentation by Ammu Abraham, activist, Women's Centre in Seminar, *Women, Politics and Religion* (Baroda, 1996).

is challenged, by presenting singleness as a viable choice and a possibly enriching way of life.[6] Activists in the Women's Centre also spend much energy attempting to retrieving the property and dowry of women experiencing domestic violence from their marital families (Women's Centre 1994, 3).

As we have seen, in the early years of the Women's Centre, there was an overlap between FAOW and Women's Centre, which created its own complexities, and tensions, leading to a split between the two groups in May 1987. Informal conversations with members of FAOW and the Women's Centre have yielded varied interpretations of events ranging from personality clashes to ideological differences between the role of 'experience' in work on domestic violence to a conflicts between activists who had experienced domestic violence and those who were in 'good marriages'. Efforts to raise these issues in formal interviews were met with reluctance, and while interviewees agreed to have their views reported, were reluctant to be named.[7] Therefore the 2 organisations are now distinct, with FAOW working primarily on advocacy, and working within an autonomous structure, with no funding and Women's Centre, working primarily with survivors of domestic violence within a more formal structure.

Left-wing response to feminisms: Stree Jagruti Samiti

As we have seen FAR was made up of a range of women, some representing organised left politics. With FAOW replacing FAR, the issue based coalition of diverse groups and individuals ended, and left political groups found themselves needing to respond to challenges faced by autonomous feminist organisations. 'Women's issues' could no longer be publicly be acknowledged as unimportant, and left-wing groups were forced to respond to this challenge by in some cases, creating and in others, strengthening their own women's wing.

Stree Jagruti Samiti was formed in 1982, by a group of Marxist-Leninist activists, some of whom had been a part of Forum Against Rape. Activists from Stree Jagruti Samiti have pointed to perceived differences between the radical feminist politics of FAR and FAOW that they disagreed with:

> Forum Against Rape and FAOW used slogans like "All men are potential rapists". We felt that this was not right, as it would alienate men from our struggles. So, we broke off and formed Stree Jagruti Samiti.[8]

While there is little evidence that such slogans were actually used (see, for instance Gothoskar 1980; Datar 1988, 23); it would appear that the primary area of difference between Stree Jagruti Samiti and FAOW appears to be in the areas and focus of

---

6   Based on verbal presentation by Ammu Abraham, activist, Women's Centre in Seminar, Women, Politics and Religion (Baroda, 1996).

7   Based on conversations with 6 members of FAOW and 2 from Women's Centre. Names of all the respondents are concealed on request.

8   Interview with Wilma Fernades, Stree Jagruti Samiti on 12 May1994.

work. While FAOW works primarily to combat violence against women, Stree Jagruti Samiti engage in a range of activities, primarily involving mobilising working class women to get access to ration cards or in the 1990s, BPL cards,[9] regular water supply and improved sanitary conditions. Sharing Marxist-Leninist ideologies, Stree Jagruti Samiti consider class oppression to be their central focus, and gender issues are therefore less important than class issues. Therefore, as in trade union politics, domestic violence against working class women is condoned, and there is an assumption that the primary issue for working class families is economic betterment, not domestic or sexual violence against women.

> Working class women know what it means for a man to work at a conveyer belt for 8–10 hours at a time. Unlike rich women, they are more understanding of the pressures that their husbands undergo as a result of the oppressive system. The battle has to be between classes, not the sexes.[10]

Within this understanding, working class men are constructed as victims of an oppressive system. The powers that patriarchies extend to men are ignored. The sexual division of labour and prescribed gender roles that allow men this 'outlet' for their frustrations, but not so women is not questioned. The implicit suggestion is that working class men work harder than their wives hence they deserve these concessions.

However, Stree Jagruti Samiti also works against women suffering domestic violence, and activists recounted the 'social boycott' that was initiated by the organisation against two families when newly married women were burnt to death due to dowry related conflicts:

> The Stree Jagruti activists organised some morchas at the community level. The courts did not give the women justice, the murderers were let off as they had political clout. The police helped in destroying evidence against the family...we felt that the only way out was to socially boycott the family... their shop was boycotted, they were ostracised from the community. This worked to punish the family.[11]

Therefore, as we have seen there are similarities between the methods used by a self consciously feminist group like Women's Centre and a Marxist–Leninist one like Stree Jagruti Samiti. Both use methods that draw upon community support. Neither have faith in legal methods or the legal system choosing to use non-legal methods of negotiation. Even though Stree Jagruti Samiti takes conservative stands on gender roles within the family, their activism on violence against women does not reflect

---

9   Till the early 1990s, all Indians had the right to non-means-based 'ration cards', which allowed them to get access to essential food items at a state subsidised rate through the Public Distribution System. An impact of market reforms in the 1990s led to these being replaced by means tested cards – therefore poverty assessment schemes led to the creation of Below Poverty Line (BPL) and Above Poverty Line (APL) cards.

10   Interview with Parul Kumtha, activist in Stree Jagruti Samiti on 12 March 1992.

11   Interview with Wilma Fernades, Stree Jagruti Samiti on 12 May 1994.

this attitude, as they work to protect the economic and social interests of working class women. Clearly their association with working class left politics as a whole and their work within working class areas leads them to reject what is constructed as 'radical feminism' as it is conceived as being alienating, and threatening to the social fabric of working class families. However, organisations such as the Women's Centre, due to their decision to work with working class women primarily on violence against women, and to locate themselves geographically 'outside' the working class community allows them more flexibility in challenging patriarchies with these communities. What is significant is that in both these cases, the focus is working with working-class women, rather than middle-class women; the challenge therefore is primarily to working class families and patriarchal structures.

Minority Feminisms

As we have seen in the previous sections, leftist groups have accused feminists of prioritising gender over class. Feminism has also been challenged by feminists from minority communities, who suggest that 'mainstream' feminism is upper caste, Hindu in its orientation; hence the issues of minority women are not addressed (FAOW 1990; Sangari 1995, 3787), leading to the formation of organisations such as Awaaz-e-Niswaan (The Voice of Women) formed in 1987 in Mumbai in a predominantly Muslim dominated area. As we will see throughout the book, the Muslim community has experienced structural economic and social discrimination, communal violence and is subjected to personal laws that have been considered discriminatory to Muslim women.[12]

Awaaz-e-Niswaan emerged from the experiences of Shahnaaz Shaikh, a Muslim woman, who was an active member of Women's Centre and FAOW in the 1980s. She had been married to Abdul Rab Ravish in 1981, who was 17 years older than her, and had subjected her to mental and physical abuse through the course of their marriage. He divorced her orally in 1983, and threw her out of the matrimonial home, without giving her the *mehr* set at Rs. 12,000 (£150). Shaikh filed a petition against the Union of India as the first respondent, and Abdul Rab Ravish as the second respondent, laying the responsibility for her oppression primarily on the Indian State suggesting that the state had failed in its responsibilities to her by not enacting fair laws for Muslim women. The petition stated:

...Respondent No. 1 has not deemed it proper or necessary to make any laws to ensure social justice for Muslim women and have restricted themselves to law making only for Hindus, Christians and for Scheduled Castes and Tribes. The Petitioner says that the Respondent No. 1 is fully aware that Muslim women constitute over 4 crores in number and are a weaker section of the Indian society. A careful and unbiased research into the

---

12 Hindus, Muslims, Parsees and Christians are governed by different personal laws governing marriage, divorce, inheritance, guardianship and adoption. Hindu personal law has been reformed in the 1950s, while Muslim Personal Law has not been amended since the middle-19th century. See Chapter 3 for more details.

various provisions of law affecting Muslim women would easily reveal the need for social reform and balancing legislation (Shahnaz Shaikh v. The Union of India and Adbul Rab Kavish 1983, 3).

The petition held that Islamic faith and legal provisions needed to be separated, as one could be a believer and yet not believe in the validity of MPL, as prescribed by the Indian State. Shaikh submitted that as a Muslim woman, she had been discriminated against by the State, who had failed in its duty to give equal rights to all Indian women (Shahnaz Shaikh v. The Union of India and Adbul Rab Kavish 1983, 6–10). The petition led to personal attacks against Shahnaz Shaikh by Muslim fundamentalist groups and individuals, forcing her to go into hiding. In addition, she found to her dismay that her lawyer was a member of the Hindu rightwing organisation RSS, who wanted to use her case to malign Islam, and the Muslim community (Menon 1994, 174). Shahnaaz's sharp and valid criticism of the Indian state was coopted by rival communal forces, and she also found herself isolated within the women's movement.

> ...even within the women's movement, I felt my minority status, felt that this is Hindu feminism. They were all very nice people, but they were not trying to understand me (cited in Menon 1994, 174).

Shahnaaz's isolation from within the movement and her community led her to withdraw her petition, and she now felt that change in MPL should come from within the community, as appeals to the state vitiated the debate. In 1987, she started Awaaz-e-Niswaan, where debates on the rights of Muslim women were carried out in terms of women's rights, attempting therefore to 'avoid the the religious framework' (Menon 1994, 174).

In the late 1980s, Awaaz-e-Niswaan was based in a small office in a Muslim dominated area, and was made up of Shaikh and a few other volunteers. Shaikh has since left the organisation, but in the early twenty-first century, Awaaz-e-Niswaan is a structured organisation with 8 full time members of staff, and regular funding. It works on diverse issues, including domestic violence, training and education for Muslim girls and women, communalism and networks with local (FAOW), national (Muslim Women's Rights Network) and international (Women Living Under Muslim Law) feminist groups. Activists in the group have experienced several attacks from community leaders, who project them as maligning the faith, and this situation is exacerbated by the proximity of the organisation to the community.[13]

---

13 Interview with Hasina Khan, Awaaz-e-Niwaan on 11 February 2005. See Chapter 3 and Chapter 6 for detailed discussions on the role of the organisation on MPL and domestic violence.

Social welfare groups: The women's question in Annapurna Mahila Mandal

This section will look at the ways in which a self consciously 'social welfare' organisation working with working class women has conceptualised and worked within Indian feminisms. One such organisation is the Annapurna Mahila Mandal (henceforth AMM) in Bombay, that emerged from the need to mobilise working class women and families in ways that differ from those adopted by Marxist Leninist groups like Stree Jagruti Samiti, or self consciously feminist ones such as Women's Centre or FAOW. AMM was founded in 1975 by Prema Purao, a CPI trade unionist who was frustrated by the marginalisation of women within left-wing trade unions. The economic shifts during the 1970s had led to the retrenchment of women workers from cotton mills, leading to the women seeking employment as khananwalis.[14] As per folklore, Annapurna is a woman who takes charge of the household and provides for the whole world after her husband deserts her. This image has a powerful resonance in the lives of the khananwalis, many of whom are forced to support their families due to absent, indifferent or unemployed husbands.

Purao attempted to organise khananwalis, who in spite of their close links with the cotton mills, have been treated as insignificant by trade unions. The most glaring problem faced by such women is an inability to get loans from nationalised banks, leading to dependence on private moneylenders, who charged high interest on the loans. AMM has helped khananwali women to create a corpus of funds on the basis of which they are able to get loans on rates of interest which are lower than those charged by private money lenders. In addition to providing credit to working class women, AMM also intervenes in situations of marital violence and discord, and encourage women to use family planning methods as a means to improve their lives:

> Many of these women are voluntarily coming out to have sterilisations done. Previously, they could never find time to go for an operation, since it meant a month's rest. Now, with the lump-sum of money, she can hire help for a month, while she recuperates from the operation (Purao cited in Savara, nd:13).

Implicit in this statement is the knowledge that many women are aware of the benefits of birth control, but have been unable to use these methods due to paucity of time, money or opportunity. AMM has helped them to identify this as a problem and to find solutions. The focus of the group is to draw out the strength already present in women, but not to question the power relations within the family:

> We do not want to create divisions within the family, though we want the lives of women to improve...we are a non political group and deal with the families and women.[15]

---

14 The term 'khananwali' literally means the provider of food. It refers to a category of women in Bombay, who have cooked meals for single working men in Bombay on a regular basis.

15 Interview with Prema Purao on 11 October 1991.

Working with families and women involves in many cases, offering women advice in cases of marital discord to to keep the family going by providing unconditional love and support. Therefore the aim of AMM is to make women economically independent, but not to challenge the oppression of women within the family.

As we have seen, groups like the AMM, and Stree Jagruti Samiti are uncomfortable with feminist politics and ideology. While women associated with these groups are empowered by their activities, often in startling ways, the focus of these groups is elsewhere – to strengthen the family, to empower working class struggles etc. Yet, as members of these groups testify, the experience of belonging to such groups can by itself be a source of great strength and accord to women some degree of control and power within the family. Women are able to meet other women in similar situations, which breaks their sense of isolation. They also gain a certain status within the community, due to their associations with the group (Gangoli 1992, 141–145).

Conclusions

As we will see in the rest of the book, most of the groups I have been discussing at some length in the preceding section, and several others, have an important, though troubled relationship with law. Campaigns around issues as varied as rape, domestic violence, sexual harassment and representation of women in the media are primarily seen through a legal prism. To some extent, this is perhaps inevitable, given that the first major feminist campaign in the 1980s was around the rape of a poor, tribal girl by the police and the acquittal of the rapists by the apex court. That is, from its inception, a challenge was posed by feminists to the courts and the police – the two vital links to the Criminal Justice System.

Several activists and feminist researchers have criticised the almost exclusive focus on legal reforms and campaigns from within the movement. There are many layers to this critique. At one level, there is the feeling that most legal reforms do not reflect the needs of the majority of Indian women. The belief in some sections is that the exigencies of survival for poor women overtakes their desire for justice, a concept at once abstract and out of reach:

> Go to a slum and talk about water or land and women will most eagerly and militantly come forward. But, speak about rights, beating, marital rape, desertion– they don't want to talk about it. How would it help them? They are more preoccupied with survival than understanding and talking about what is rightfully theirs (women's movement activist from Bangalore, cited in Gandhi and Shah 1989, 259).

Another aspect of the AWM that has been critiqued – both within and outside the movement – is the question of funding. Most feminist groups are entirely or predominantly dependent on funding from western funding agencies. Left-wing parties and trade unions have pointed out that foreign funding has had a severe impact on the nature, and content of the movement by pushing feminists into areas that are defined by the agenda of the funder, which can subvert radical politics, as issues are defined from outside, rather than from within the movement (Bhrame et. al. 1987, 7–9).

While the problems associated with foreign funding, and the threat of neo imperialistic cooption of the movement has been discussed at length within feminist groups and individuals, some have defended the use of foreign funding as strategic, and enabling the feminist movement to expand its base beyond a few middle class women who may have the leisure and resources to contribute their time and services to the movement. The exigencies of funding can force organisations to work more efficiently, and to employ working class women, which benefits the movement as a whole.[16] These are issues that the movement continues to grapple with, along with several others, as we will see in the following chapters.

---

16 Interview with Nandita Shah, Akshara Documentation Centre on 5 March 2001.

Chapter 3

Feminism and the State: Citizenship, Legislative Debates and Women's Issues

This chapter examines the relationship between feminism and the state through the prism of gendered debates on citizenship and women's rights. Some Indian feminists have constructed debates of equality on the basis of equal rights as citizens of the country, therefore arguing that women in India have rights equal to men because they are Indian citizens (Sangari 1995, 3788). We will examine whether this perspective meets the needs of diverse women, therefore whether discourses of citizenship are limiting for women's rights in particular and feminism in general. This will be addressed through two specific debates – debates around civil rights of Muslim women contrasted with parallel rights of Hindu majority women, therefore the marginalisation of Muslim women. Secondly, we will look at the ways in which sexualisation of women's bodies in the varied contexts of communal riots and sex work leads to their marginalisation within citizenship debates.

Being Muslim and a woman: State, community and feminist debates

Debates on personal laws and Uniform Civil Code

In India, personal laws govern different religious communities in the civil areas of marriage, divorce, maintenance, guardianship, custody and adoption. This has been conceptualised as a remnant of colonial jurisprudence, where a policy of non interference with 'personal customs' led to codification of Hindu, Christian, Parsee and Muslim Personal Laws, based on detailed discussions and consultations with representatives of religious bodies, most often men (see for instance: Singh 1993, 177–197; Kishwar 1994, 2145–2161; Lateef 1994, 56), prior to independence in 1947; and subsequent recodification of Hindu Personal Law in the 1940s after independence in the 1950s (Kishwar 1994, 2145–2161).

Personal laws have therefore been constructed as markers of identity for different religious communities. This is more so in the case of the Muslim community. This remains a shifting marker, and creates a set of images, both in the self-image of different members of the Muslim community, and in the perception of other actors including the State, different political parties, and individuals. Identity formation takes place at moments of crisis, as well as in the day-to-day events and continuing lives of women and men. However, while in the most part, the identity within and of a group may not be strong; it can become intense when there is a perceived or real threat to the interests of the group (Kakar 1995, vii–x). Some moments of crisis for the members of the Muslim community in India are the partition of India in 1947; communal riots; the demolition of the Babri Masjid in December 1992–93 and anti Muslim riots in Gujarat in 2002. I would suggest that debates centred on personal laws played a prominent role in shaping the identity of the Muslim community and the Hindu community, and this happened at specific moments of crisis, such as the Shah Bano controversy, and the ways in which members of these communities understood and articulated personal law in their daily lives.

In the 1930s, the process of codifying Muslim personal law was initiated at the behest of members of the community, and the Shariat Act, 1937, and the Dissolution of Muslim Marriages Act, 1939 were passed. The purpose of these acts was to apply Muslim Personal Law (MPL) to Muslim men and women who were governed by customary laws. In the perception of those initiating these laws, these were progressive steps, giving Muslim women rights denied to them under 'customary law'[1] The Shariat Act brought all Indian Muslims under the Shariat laws in matters related to inheritance, divorce, marriage and guardianship. The 1939 Act extended to all Muslim women rights of divorce that had so far been restricted to Hanafi Muslims (Singh 1993, 177–9), leading to the codification of MPL being seen as inspirational for other communities including the Hindu community in uplifting the status of women (Lateef 1994, 56).

However, partition, communal riots in the 1940s and independence in 1947 led to a shift in the economic, political and social status of Muslims in independent India, leading to a marginalisation of Muslim communities, that has been well documented (Lateef 1994; Kakar 1995). In the decade following independence, the political focus was on the reform of Hindu personal law, named the Hindu Code bill. The bill, which aimed to codify and reform Hindu Personal Law, faced tremendous opposition both within and outside parliament. The bill was divided into four separate parts, and passed as The Hindu Marriage Act, 1955; The Hindu Minority and Guardianship Act, 1956; The Hindu Adoption and Maintenance Act, 1956 and The Hindu Succession Act, 1955. These laws have long been presented as model laws that initiated in Indian society, progress and enlightenment. This is not the place to support or dispute these claims, which has been done elsewhere (Kishwar 1994, 2145–2161), but I would like to point out that these laws were responsible for creating an exclusionist, yet inclusive legal category of a Hindu, as a Hindu is defined as including anyone who is not a Muslim, Parsee, Christian or Jew; therefore including within its scope Jains, Sikhs, Buddhists and non Christian tribals and Dalits. It has therefore been suggested that this legal description of a Hindu, in relation with the four religions excluded to it, means that these religions become its legal 'other' (Sangari 1995, 3788–9).

---

1   Here, it may be relevant to point out that the term 'customary law' has never been defined in the legislature, it is taken to mean conventions and usage adhered to by people for a long period of time (Arif, 1994).

Moreover far from creating a feminist legal system for Hindu women, these laws offer women limited rights to divorce, and includes the 'right to conjugal rights', which as we will see in Chapter 4, legitimises marital rape. As we have seen in Chapter 1, until 2005, the Hindu Succession Act, 1955 offered Hindu women limited rights over inheritance, especially over ancestral property, and it has been demonstrated that in practice Hindu women were often deprived of these limited rights through a variety of legal and social pressures (Kishwar 1993).[2] In 1955, Hindu women's restricted property rights was met with opposition in the Constituent Assembly, with members arguing that it would destroy Hindu society, and create discord between brothers and sisters. It was further argued that the government should pass a uniform civil code (UCC), and until that was done, Hindu laws should not be tampered with (Singh 1993, 187–188), therefore using the demand for a UCC as a way to postpone reforms within Hindu laws. It was argued that the Hindu code bill was 'absolutely unnecessary' and that 'it goes against the principle of having a common civil code' (Thakur Das Bhargava, cited in Kishwar 1994, 2152). Many members of the constituent assembly pushed for a UCC, on the grounds that it would facilitate national integration; others opposed it on the grounds that it would jeopardise the cultural identity of minorities, especially Muslims. This was perhaps a historic moment when the debate around UCC became petrified into a debate around individual rights, citizenship and national integration on the one hand, and minority rights, and cultural diversity on the other. A general sense of unease with these ideas held paramount till date in the struggle against British colonialism is apparent in the following excerpt from a speech made by the Prime Minister, Jawaharlal Nehru in 1949:

> Nationalism, of course, is a curious phenomenon, which at a certain stage in a country's history, gives life, growth, strength, a unity but it has the tendency to limit one ... Culture, which is essentially good, becomes not only static, but aggressive and something that breeds conflict and hatred when looked at from a wrong point of view. How you are to find a balance, I don't know (Government of India 1965, 361).

Nehru here seems to be equally critical of the limitations of nationalism, as of culture, seeing in these dangers of conflict and division. Meanwhile, sections of Muslims who had stayed back in India, following partition, felt marginalised and anxious about the ways in which Indian nationalism was being constructed, rejecting the UCC as threatening their identity as Muslims.[3]

---

2   The Hindu Succession Act 1955 was replaced by the Hindu Succession (Amendment Act) 2005 that allowed Hindu women equal rights over ancestral property. However in most cases these rights are nominal as even in the case of non-ancestral lands daughters have most often ceded their rights to inheritance to their brothers or husbands.

3   In 1950, a member of the Jamait-e-Ulema wrote an article in an Urdu newspaper, in which he warned Muslims that Hindus were basing 'their' constitution on the laws of Manu. Quoted in Karandikar (1987), 22.

The rationale for introducing a UCC on the grounds that it would contribute to 'national integration' of different communities was rejected by some members of the Constituent Assembly, since it was pointed out that existing uniform laws for crimes, contracts, torts and constitutional rights had not successfully promoted it (cited in Bhargava 1983, 11). Even some of those who held strongly to the desirability of a UCC, stopped short of making this demand legally justifiable.[4] What is clear is that the discourse around personal laws and UCC was conducted within the parameters of national integration and community rights, not those of women's rights within the family.

Between the mid 1950s to the mid 1970s, little or no debate took place on the issue of MPL in the legislature. The only effort to do so was in the 1960s, there was an unsuccessful move was made to amend MPL, which was dropped when the Vice President of India, Zakir Hussain conveyed a sense of resentment on the behalf of the entire Muslim community (Karandikar 1987, 180). Possible reasons for the silence on this issue could be the retreat of communal forces during this period, the gender indifference of the Left which seemed in ascendancy at that point and a greater focus on nation building in the specific Nehruvian mould.

Representation of MPL in legislative debates and judicial pronouncements (1975–1995)

Legislative debates during this period reveal a 'Hinduised' understanding of family life, womanhood and gender relations, within which Islamic tenets are constructed at best as aberrant and different.[5] Such imagery is apparent in the lengthy debates in the Lok Sabha in 1976, while debating the proposed amendments to the Hindu Marriage Act, 1955 (henceforth HMA) and the Special Marriage Act, 1954 (SMA).[6] The 1976 amendment is known to bring the HMA 'on par' with the SMA, but what is often disregarded is that the amendment also 'returned' to Hindu men their right

4   KM Muslim and Krishna Swami Aiyyar, ardent supporters of a UCC, as a means of strengthening nationalism, voted against the inclusion of the clause as a fundamental right, and hence legally enforceable. Munshi had made a strong statement that the failure of the state to amend personal laws of different communities would lead to a denial of rights of women. Yet, he supported the placing of the clause in the section on Directive Principles of State Policy, a legally non enforceable section. (Dhagamwar, 1989, 127).

5   For instance, a Muslim MP, Shri E S M Fakir Mohommad stated during a debate for grants to the Ministry of Social and Women's Welfare that:

'Sir, in India, we worship women as the universal Shakti; the world will not survive without women. We pay homage to our country in the name of Bharat Mata' (Lok Sabha Debates 1985, 239).

6   The HMA is the law under which marriages between two Hindus can be registered, while the SMA allows registeration of marriages between two people of any religion, including therefore inter community marriages and marriages between Indian citizens and non Indians.

to ancestral property provided they married another Hindu under the act.[7] This amendment favouring Hindu men, which served the additional purpose of making marriages between Hindu men and non Hindu women less attractive than marriages between Hindus was passed without any debate or discussion within the Parliament (Lok Sabha Debates 1976b, 160–161; Lok Sabha Debates 1976c, 8–90, Lok Sabha Debates 1976d, 8–38).

The 1976 Lok Sabha debates on the SMA and the HMA describe marriage as fitting closely to brahmanical and Hindu perceptions of marriage, while alluding to 'Indian' marriage. The following excerpt indicates this trend:

> According to Indian culture and tradition, marriage is a sacred and eternal bond. When a man and a woman enter into marriage, our culture and civilisation tells them that only death can separate the two (Shri Chandra Shailani, Lok Sabha Debates 1976c: 85. Translated from Hindi).

The elision between 'Hindu' high caste understanding of marriage[8] and 'Indian' marriage indicates that a number of assumptions are made about what it means to be Indian, and by extension an Indian citizen. There is a link, by no means tenuous between these notions of society and marriage, and those carried out a decade later in the Lok Sabha prior to the passing of the Muslim Women (Protection of Rights Upon Marriage) Act, 1986. In the 1986 debates, several MPs expressed a discomfort with how they perceived Islamic marriage, constructed as different and therefore inferior to 'Hindu' marriages.

> Now, the law of Muslims relating to marriage and divorce is this...Marriage is a matter of contract...it is not a sacrament at all. A woman is not married to a man till eternity, as it was with the Hindus and as it was with Catholics in the olden days...to the Muslims, divorce was very much known... (Shri A.K. Sen, Lok Sabha Debates 1986a, 315).

One MP held it fitting to issue a warning to all Muslims to transform themselves:

> I would like to warn the Muslims also. They have made divorce a very ordinary and easy thing. Recognise the need of the hour and change yourself (Smt Vidyavati Chaturvedi, Lok Sabha Debates 1986a, 471).

While much debate in the Parliament revealed the extent of stereotypical representations of Muslims, there were some feminist responses to, and critiques of Islamic practices that looked at the ways in which women were discriminated against in Islamic divorce. For instance, MP Geeta Mukherjee argued that:

---

7   This right had been denied to them under the act in 1954, when it had been ruled that any person marrying under this act would be governed by the Indian Succession Act, 1925. This had meant that Hindu men would lose their right to ancestral property.

8   For more details on Brahmanical notions of Hindu marriage, see Fruzzetti (1993).

When an Islamic marriage takes place, (the) woman's consent is necessary. But, please remember, at the time of divorce, the divorced woman's consent is not at all necessary (Lok Sabha Debates 1986a, 424).

There is only one recorded protest to the communalisation of the debates, a protest that was not acknowledged or responded to:

The Law Minister talks about Muslim representatives (in the Lok Sabha)...no one is a Hindu representative or a Muslim representative in this house...He is communalising the whole issue (Shri Saifuddin Chaudhry, Lok Sabha Debates 1986a, 364).

The Muslim Women's Bill   The Muslim Women's Bill was introduced in the wake of nationwide movements by different interest groups following the controversial 'Shah Bano' judgement. The issue of maintenance to divorced Muslim women was politicised in the mid-1980s following a Supreme Court case regarding a divorced Muslim woman's right under Section 125 of the Criminal Procedure Code (henceforth Cr.PC) to claim maintenance (Mohommed Ahmed Khan v. Shah Bano Begum and Others 1985).[9] The details of the case are as follows. Shah Bano filed for maintenance in the Court of Judicial Magistrate after she was abandoned by her husband and thrown out of the matrimonial home after thirty years of marriage. Following this, she was divorced by her husband who maintained that he was had paid her mehr and was therefore not entitled to pay her any more maintenance under MPL. The Magistrate awarded maintenance under S125 Cr.PC to the effect of Rs. 25 per month, and this sum was enhanced to Rs. 179.20[10] on appeal to the High Court. The husband appealed to the Supreme Court, stating that he was not entitled to pay her maintenance following the divorce under MPL.

On the surface, the Supreme Court judgment on the surface appeared to make a valid legal point, that Section 125 Cr.PC was a part of the criminal law of the country, hence was applicable to all Indians. However, the judge also made a number of contentious remarks about Islamic law, citing a statement made by Sir William in 1843 that the fatal point in Islam was its degradation of women, thereby stating that:

It is a matter of regret that article 44[11] of our constitution has remained a dead letter... a common civil code will help the cause of national integration by removing disparate loyalties to laws that have conflicting ideologies. (Mohommed Ahmed Khan v. Shah Bano Begum and Others 1985, 945).

As we will see later, several contesting groups were involved in the issue: the Hindu right, who saw this as an ideal opportunity to lash out at the 'backwardness' of

---

9   Section 125 Cr. PC is a part of criminal law, the purpose of the section being that to prevent destitution. Under this section, the 'destitute' person was entitled to relief to the maximum amount of Rs. 500.

10   At current rates, Rs 80 equals one pound (sterling).

11   Article 44 is the Directive Principle of State Policy that directs the Indian State to create a Uniform or common civil code.

the Muslims. Muslim fundamentalist groups, who felt that Shah Bano's claim for maintenance post divorce was 'un-Islamic'; Muslim intellectuals and liberals who disagreed with this interpretation of MPL and left-wing parties and feminists, who wanted this issue to be addressed in terms of women's rights (Das 1995, 85–117). The debate also revealed the divisions within the Muslim community (Hasan 1998). It has been suggested that within the narratives of the Shah Bano case, the 'Muslim woman question' was displaced onto different discourses; and these were unified by 'the assumptions of an ideology of protection' of the Muslim woman (Pathak and Sunder Rajan 1989, 562).

The Lok Sabha debates bring out the concerns of the Indian State to attempt to conciliate some of these demands:

> Sir, you know, some time ago, a meeting of the Muslim women was held at the Boat Club – not our meeting, but their meeting. Our people went there also, fundamentalists told them that the government is going to give money to the wakf boards, Rs. 50 crores, and the CPI(M) is opposing that ((Shri Saifuddin Chaudhry, Lok Sabha Debates 1986a, 364).

The Bill aimed at bringing Muslim women exclusively within the ambit of MPL, and outside the criminal law on maintenance, was defended by many MPs belonging to the ruling Congress Party that had introduced the bill, as being based on the understanding of MPL shared by what was understood as the Muslim community.

> If this (the bill) is the understanding of the Muslims of their own personal laws, the government is duty bound to pay attention...(and) not to impose something on them (Shri A.K. Sen, Lok Sabha Debates 1986a, 317).

While the ruling party posed the issue in terms of the cultural rights and practices of the Muslim community, some sections of the opposition opposed the bill on the grounds of the rights of Muslim women. However, the language used by both sections was not dissimilar to feminist rhetoric. The following extracts, the first from a supporter of the bill, the second from an opponent, use the language of rights, women's self-respect and modernity:

> The (Shah Bano) judgment has let down the women in the society. ... Why a self respecting woman will go to a person who has divorced her and thrown her out of his house, to beg maintenance for herself? (Smt. Abida Ahmed, Lok Sabha Debates 1986a, 418).

> Muslim women went to the Prime Minister with tears in their eyes. One Muslim girl said, 'Mr. Prime Minister, for the third time, I have been offered talaq. And if you are talking in terms of going to the twenty-first century, why do you want to throw ladies like us to the sixth century?' (Shri Madhu Dandavate, Lok Sabha Debates 1986a, 380).

Ahmed and Dandavate, from opposing viewpoints, aim to legitimise and strengthen their positions using the experiences of women, their rights and the oppression meted out to them in a male dominated world. That women's concerns, and the rhetoric of Indian feminists have been assimilated within the concerns of the State is on the one hand, an achievement; signifying that feminist politics have been, to some extent, mainstreamed. However, some feminists believe that this is little more than a cooption of feminist language for narrow political gain (Gothoskar et. al. 1994, 3020).

However, the State cannot be collapsed with the interests of one or the other political party. There are several conflicting interests that the State has to look into, negotiate and try to reach a consensus. Indeed in other contexts it has been suggested that the state is a part of struggles within society and that state activity grows out of the irreconciliabilty of conflicts within society (Eisentein 1993, 225–231). In this case, the Indian State perhaps sought to resolve the diverse pulls of feminist politics, democratic and secular left-wing forces, Hindu communal parties and Muslim liberals and Muslim fundamentalist bodies. In addition, the ruling Congress-I government had in late 1985 suffered an electoral defeat in a by-election in a Muslim dominated area, and this was attributed to Muslim discontent with the Shah Bano judgement. That the bill could only satisfy one section – Muslim communal forces – and leftist disgruntled various other interest groups, feminists, democratic and liberal forces, Hindu communal parties, indicates the complexities of the political scene with which Indian politicians were attempting to grapple with at that point in Indian history, and as Hasan suggests points to ways in which the Indian State ignored the divisions and internal fissures within the Muslim community, and Muslim women (1998). The Lok Sabha debates had focused on community rights, i.e. the rights of minority communities to self regulate their personal laws (where the community was represented by men) rather than the rights of Indian Muslim women as equal citizens entitled to equal protection under the law. The contract, unofficial as it was, between the state, the community and the household, was based on patriarchal interests, therefore working to the detriment of women within the community.

Judicial interpretations   Judges have responded to, and contributed to the public debates on MPL and UCC in various cases on maintenance, divorce, polygamy, guardianship and inheritance. As we have seen, the Shah Bano judgment raised a furore within the Muslim community, and in general raised the question of the relationship between 'secular law' and the rights of minorities and the rights of women (Das 1995, 93). What is significant, however, is the general political context within which the controversy grew. This was certainly not the first judgment supported the rights of Muslim divorcees to maintenance under Section 125 CrPC (Bai Tahira v. Ali Hussein Fissalli Chothia and Another 1979, 362), but the communalised ambiance of the mid-1980s (Varney 2002) could potentially have contributed to the responses that the Shah Bano judgement created. The Shah Bano judgement therefore became the site where immense conflict between Hindu and Muslim leaders was played out, with Hindu communal leaders representing the judgement as a positive step for Indian secularism, and Muslim fundamentalist leaders opposing it on the grounds of state interference in community and domestic matters. Shah Bano, unable to bear the pressures exerted on her from within the community, recanted in an open letter to Muslims. The letter, poignant in its helplessness, reads:

Maulana Mohommad Habib Yar Khan, Haji Abdul Gaffar Sahib and other respectable gentlemen of Indore came to me and explained the commands concerning nikaah, divorce, dower and maintenance in the light of the Quran and the hadith ... Now, the Supreme Court of India has given the judgment on 23 April 1985 concerning maintenance of the divorced woman, which apparently is in my favour. But since the judgment is contrary to the Quran and the hadith and is an open interference in Muslim Personal Law, I, Shah Bano, being a Muslim, reject it and disassociate myself from every judgment that is contrary to the Shariat (Shah Bano, 1985).

Shah Bano's withdrawal from the controversy is an example of what has been described as 'intersectionality' i.e. the way in which multiple identities – in this case, gender and religion – cut across each other to advantage or, as in this case, disadvantage particular individuals and groups in society (Hootge and Koos Kingma 2004, 47–55). Shah Bano's status as a woman within a minority community that felt itself under threat, meant that when the state supported her rights, the support created repercussions within the community that forced her to reject her rights.

As we have seen, the ruling Congress Party gave in to the pressures exerted by the more orthodox within the Muslim community, passing the Muslim Women (Protection of Rights Upon Marriage) Act, 1986, that removed divorced Muslim women from the ambit of Section 125 CrPC, choosing to focus on one time relief to divorced women. Significantly, the voices of those members of the community who had supported the rights of Muslim women to maintenance under the CrPC was ignored, including a memorandum submitted to the Prime Minister signed by several members of the community, who distanced itself from those members of the community who opposed the judgment and stated:

We believe that Muslim women have the right to maintenance – a right that they enjoy in several Muslim countries, through the rational and progressive interpretation of Islamic principles, as in Morocco, Iraq, Egypt, Turkey, Libya, Tunisia, Syria and Algeria....We emphasize the necessity of safeguarding the interests of all sections of the minorities. That is why the demand to exclude Muslim women from the purview of section 125 Cr P C... would adversely affect both the rights and interests of Muslim women. (Memorandum cited in Engineer 1978, 217–221).

Similarly, following the enactment of the Muslim Women (Protection of Rights Upon Marriage) Act, 1986, two advocates, who identified themselves as members of the Muslim community, filed a writ petition in the Supreme Court, stating that the Act was discriminatory and 'calculated to disrupt and divide the most exploited and vulnerable section of our people', submitting that the act be struck down on various grounds, including that it violated the right to equality before the law and equal protection of the law guaranteed under the constitution, that it would encourage divorce and female infanticide, thus militating against 'two of the causes to which the Holy Prophet of Islam dedicated a great part of his life' (Latifi and Khan v. The Union of India 1986). The petition combined religious and secular arguments to oppose the law that was passed, which was based simultaneously on Muslim women's rights as citizens entitled to equal treatment under the law and on traditions of reform within Islam supporting the rights of women.

Equally remarkably, the Hindu right wing party, BJP opposed the 1986 act on the grounds that it violated the rights of Muslim women. In an official statement made in 1986, the act was called 'retrograde, anti women and a surrender to obscurantism and bigotry' (BJP 1986). This is especially ironical given the anti feminist and anti Muslim politics of the BJP, that is manifested as we will see later, in anti Muslim pogroms in Mumbai in 1992, and in Gujarat in 2002 where sexual violence against Muslim women was actively carried out and condoned by the BJP (International Initiative for Justice in Gujarat 2003).

It might be useful to look at the interpretations of the 1986 Act, to assess the impact that this law has had on Muslim women. Some of the judgments based on this act have tried to interpret it as liberally as possible, in order to provide a fair settlement for divorced Muslim women.[12] In 1995, Justice TV Ramakrishnan of the Kerala High court dismissed the petition of K Haji who pleaded that the maintenance amount of Rs. 30, 000 as one time settlement after divorce granted to Amina, his ex-wife by the Sessions Court was illegal under the 1986 act, on the grounds that the act granted 'reasonable and fair provision' and maintenance during the period of *iddat*. In an earlier case, the Gujarat High court had ruled that the 1986 act provided for fair settlement according to the financial status of the husband. Justice M B Shah ruled that:

> Under S 125 Cr P C, the maximum amount which a divorced woman would get is only Rs. 500, even though her former husband is a rich person. Therefore to give her full protection or benefit, this Act is enacted and her rights are specified...It has not only provided for free and fair provision and maintenance to the divorced woman and her minor children, but it has also specifically provided that she is entitled to get mehr or dower amount from her former husband (Arab Ahemadhia Abdulla v. Arab Bail Mohmuna Saiyadbhai. 1988, 141).

Therefore this judgement provides an alternative legal understanding of the Muslim Women's Law, that it is designed to protect and benefit Muslim women, and feeds into the view, held by some lawyers, activists and litigants that a one-time settlement is more beneficial fof women than regular monthly payments in maintenance cases. Therefore we can see that the 1986 act does benefit Muslim women when interpreted by a pro-woman judge. However, in its very conception it remains discriminatory against Muslim women, as it denies a section of women access to a secular law on the grounds of their religion.

If the mid-1980s were taken over by legal debates on maintenance and divorce, the issues under debate in the 1990s were those of oral divorce under Muslim law and

---

12   Under Section 125 Cr PC, as we have seen, the maintenance amount awarded was most often very small, there being a ceiling of Rs. 500. See for instance Shahzadi Begum v. Mohommad Abdul Gaffar 1981, 1532, where the maintenance amount was Rs 75 (one pound sterling).

polygamy. The issue of *talaq-e-biddat*, known more popularly as triple *talaq*, has been constructed as the marker of negative Muslim identity by Hindu fundamentalists. In 1993, Justice Tilhari of the Uttar Pradesh High Court struck down *talaq-e-biddat* as invalid, while commenting on the joys of marriage, the sorrows of divorce, and the 'plight' of a Muslim divorced woman:

> ...marriage is a status which creates vested rights and interest of cohabitation, succession and maintenance. It brings a bloom to the life. Divorce brings a plight of vagaries...and upheaval in the life of a woman...The Hindu Marriage Act introduced divorce and a divorced woman has been declared to be 'entitled to claim maintenance from her husband'. Under Muslim law, the plight of a woman divorced by her husband is more pathetic. It is the husband who has the free hand to divorce his wife....even orally, by declaring talaq thrice...the poor Muslim woman has been held to be entitled to maintenance for a limited period of three months and then left to the vagaries of fate (Rahmatullah v. State of UP, Khatoonisa v. State of UP 1993)

The judgement declared 'triple talaq' both as unconstitutional, and as sinful under the mandate of the Holy Quran. While accepting that 'triple talaq' was unIslamic, Justice Tilhari continued to conceptualise the issue in terms the 'superiority' of Hindu laws and cultural practices over Muslim law and marriage practice, and to reiterate the centrality of marriage as an institution.

Justice Kuldip Singh's judgment in a case on bigamy in 1995 raised similar issues. The case was that of a Hindu man, who converted to Islam in order to solemnise a second marriage. The Supreme Court judgment speculated about MPL, comparing it unfavourably with Hindu law, and advised the Parliament to enact a UCC so as to prevent cases such as these. He ruled that:

> The personal law of the Hindus, such as relating to marriage, succession and the like have a sacramental origin, in the same manner as in the case of the Muslims or the Christians. The Hindus, along with Sikhs, Buddhists and Jains have forsaken their sentiments in the cause of national unity and integration, some other communities would not, though the constitution enjoins the establishment of a common civil code for the whole of India (Sarla Mudgal and Others v. the Union of India and Others 1995, 351).

Justice Singh felt that a common civil code would prevent Hindu men from converting to Islam in order to escape the provisions of their personal laws, which would penalise them for bigamy. The stated purpose of the proposed common laws was therefore, to 'save' Hindu marriages, not to protect Muslim women from ill effects of polygamy (Sarla Mudgal and Others v. the Union of India and Others 1995, 351). Elsewhere, it has been argued that the Hindu Marriage Act, 1955, while technically disallowing polygamous marriages, has not been very effective in doing so, due to loopholes in the marriage law that recognise as valid only one kind of Hindu marriage, for example, the high caste Brahminical marriage including the *saptapadi*, leaving out a range of customary marriages practiced by members of different caste groups. Hindu men have used this clause with impunity by entering into second or third marriages which are based on customary marriage practices not recognised under HMA, to deny the wives rights due to them. Therefore, feminist lawyers have argued that the loopholes in the HMA allow Hindu men 'to escape the criminal consequences of a bigamous marriage, and from the economic responsibility towards the second wife' (Agnes 1995, 3238). This judgement on bigamy, has however been appropriated by Hindu communal forces, not unlike the Shah Bano and the Tilhari judgments before it. Therefore, a unsuccessful bill initiated by the Hindu right wing Shiv Sena-BJP combine in Maharashtra in 1995 to prevent bigamous marriages among all communities in the state quotes approvingly from the judgement in its statement of objects and reasons (LA Bill No. XXXII of 1995).

It might be relevant to point out that the bias against MPL in legislative, legal and judicial discourses on the UCC becomes even more apparent from the absence of discussion or debate about the areas of MPL that might be considered pro women, such as inheritance rights. Under MPL, Muslim women have rights to parental property, and married women have rights over their husbands' property, and they cannot be disinherited through a will (Multiple Action Research Group and Women and Child Development 1992).

Feminist responses to MPL

Feminists have been involved in debates around personal laws, and rights of Muslim women since the 1950s (see for example, Dhagamwar 1989, 44–66; Singh 1993, 177–197; Kishwar, 1994, 2145–2161). In 1974, the Status of Women Report commissioned by the Indian government, and written by a group of feminist activists recognised that Muslim men enjoyed more rights than Muslim women, while simultaneously acknowledging both the limitations of legal reform, and the need for legal change:

> Legislation alone can not eliminate rigid traditionalism, with its desire to preserve the status quo....(however) legislation is the only instrument which can bring the Muslim divorce law into line with not only the needs of society, but with the prevailing laws in other Muslim countries (Guha et. al. 1974, 121–2).

The Status of Women Report recommended the elimination of unilateral right of divorce for Muslim men, and the extension of maintenance for Muslim women, while acknowledging the superiority of MPL over the personal laws of other communities in the area of inheritance rights for women:

> Muslim law makes no distinction between movable and immovable property, and the rights of a female heir, unlike a widow or daughter has always been recognised, and they have inherited absolutely (unlike the old Hindu law) (Guha et. al. 1974, 140).

The authors of the report concluded that there was an urgent need to implement a UCC, on the grounds of national integration, modernisation and gender parity, suggesting that the absence of a Uniform Civil Code was 'an incongruity that can not be justified with all the emphasis that is placed on secularism, science and modernisation' (Guha et. al. 1974, 140) and that personal laws that discriminated between genders were both unconstitutional and 'against the spirit of national integration and secularism' (Guha et. al. 1974, 140).

The rhetoric of women's rights therefore was connected to national integration and modernity, equality therefore understood in the terms as sameness between communities. As we have seen in Chapter 2, Shahnaz Shaikh's petition challenging the Indian nation (Shahnaz Shaikh v. The Union of India and Adbul Rab Kavish 1983,). acknowledged the ways in which 'intersectionality' of gender and faith had adversely affected her, but her appeal was made directly to her rights as a citizen of the country, rather than as a member of a minority community. The withdrawal of the petition in Shaikh's case (as in Shah Bano's) was linked to the recognition of the potential for cooption of women's rights' rhetoric by fundamentalist – and inherently misogynist – forces. Unlike Shah Bano however, Shaikh continued to work towards women's rights, however now accepting that changes within MPL should come from within the community, as appeals to the state communalised the debate. Therefore in the feminist collective started by Shaikh in 1987, the UCC were rephrased as 'women's code', which was seen as a way to 'avoid the religious framework' that would paralyse discussion (Menon 1994, 174). However her conviction that work needed to be done within the community to reform MPL did not detract from her belief that Islam has its limitations as far as women's rights are concerned (Menon 1994, 174).

Other feminists and activists within the Muslim community in India, and elsewhere, have argued for feminist reinterpreting of the Quran, and there have been suggestions that Islam offers unlimited scope for gender reform, based on the Quranic injunction that 'women have rights similar to those of men' and that any anomalies that have crept into law are the result of misrepresentation.[13] This view has informed the efforts of a Bombay based group called the Nikaahnama Group, made up of Muslim women who are self identified as feminists, and has created a model nikaahnama (marriage contract) on the basis of which women can claim rights to matrimonial property, some safeguards from unilateral divorce and polygamy, and provisions that entitle women to maintenance at divorce based on the financial status of the man and right to an enhanced mehr in the case of unilateral divorce. It also states that the permission of the first wife be taken if the man wants to contract a second marriage, and in the case of subsequent marriages, the permission of all the wives be taken.[14]

At one level, this prism does have its positive aspects, as it could potentially enable Muslim women to evolve a feminist understanding of practices and laws,

---

13   Asghar Ali Engineer, Women and Muslim Law. Presentation at Consultation on Gender Just Laws. Organised by Forum Against Oppression of Women, Lawyers' Collective and Human Rights Law Network, Bombay. 5–8 June, 1996.

14   Oral Presentations by Vahida Nainar and Nahida Sheikh at Seminar on Reforms in Law. Organised by Women's Centre, Bombay. March 1996. The 'model nikaahnama' has been used in two marriages held in February 2006 in Mumbai.

without alienating the men in the community. However, the debate becomes restricted to the terms ones set by the community, and the texts under study. To elaborate, the model Nikaahnama has no provisions for women who do not enter into marriage. Besides, feminists have suggested that the provisions to 'regulated' polygamy in the nikaahnama are inadequate and unjust, on the grounds that the responsibility to 'prevent' polygamous marriages cannot be given to vulnerable women, who are often economically dependent on their husbands. It has also been suggested that at a conceptual level, regulated polygamy is unfair unless it is accompanied by regulated polyandry (Hensmen 1987, 4–7). In addition, Muslim feminists found in 2005 that their 'model nikaahnama' based on gender equality was ignored by the All India Muslim Personal Law Board, whose version of the nikaahnama did not mention rights of the first wife in cases of polygamy, or provide for a woman's right to divorce or set a mehr amount that would appreciate with inflation. In addition the nikaahnama of the Muslim Personal Law Board increases the role and authorities of the Shariat courts that known for their anti feminist stance (Seshu 2005). As the All India Muslim Personal Law Board carries more influence in the community and with the State, the efforts of Muslim feminists have been negated.

Within the women's movement, there have been some criticisms of the 'reform from within' position, suggesting that this form of legal pluralism is based on the primordial identity of community, and is thus antithetical to feminism.

> I believe that a feminism which is based on a critique of biologism and on the sexual division of labour rests, definitionally, on the right to chosen political affiliation and privileges social identities...above birth bound ones, it can not flirt uncritically with primordialism. Primordial claims can not be a feminist principle, because they are a principle of irrevocable distention, and will divide women by region, caste, religion and race (Sangari 1995, 3289).

The argument has parallels with Gellner's hypothesis that 'modularity' or the ability to rise beyond 'traditional' or ascriptive occupations and associations is the mark of civil society, while 'segmentation' defines a traditional society, where there is no freedom of will with regard to associations, occupation or place of residence. Such a 'segmented' society might avoid the tyranny of the state, because of decentralisation of production, low level of communication technology or the self sufficiency of each segment, but would experience a 'tyranny of cousins', as it thrusts upon the individual an ascribed identity, rather than a chosen one. Gellner concludes that civil society is not only modern, but also based on strictly voluntary, not ethnic or religious associations between the family and the state (Gellner 1995). Sangari's (and Gellner's) critique of 'traditional' societies explains the patriarchal control that women such as Shah Bano and Shahnaz Shaikh have to suffer from members of the community, while rejecting rights that the 'secular' State could offer them.

However, the argument glosses over the context within which women live their lives, suggesting that an allegiance to feminism, defined in somewhat monolithic terms, means an automatic break with all that is defined as 'primordial', that is region, caste, religion and race. We have seen that women within minority situations, in this case, Muslim women work hard to balance their feminist politics with their religious identity, attempting as in the case of the Nikaahnama Group to amend both. Women like Shaikh do not 'flirt uncritically' with community ties, rather they accept the limitations of community patriarchy and of monolithic feminism. Therefore, attachment to religious identity does not necessarily preclude a feminist orientation.

As we have seen there are within the women's movement, multiple perceptions of the issue of reform of MPL. On the one hand, are the efforts of groups like Awaaz-e-Niswaan and the Nikaahnama Group who work to internally reform MPL, through work within the community. Then, there are the perceptions that the debate should be articulated primarily in terms of women's rights, though in a shift from earlier debates, not in terms of national integration or 'sameness':

> We believe that...a religion wise categorization (of personal laws) tends to become inward looking, and leads to the logic of internal reforms. It also detracts from the inadequacies and discrimination that all women face and share in common (Gandhi and Shah 1992, 229).

Another solution to the issue of civil rights for women can be seen in the position adopted by a Delhi based group, Working Group for Women's Rights (henceforth WGWR), who in 1995, recommended the creation of a comprehensive package of legislation that would embody gender justice, including equal family laws, as well as equal laws in employment. This package would be available to all men and women in the country, yet they can choose allegiance to personal laws in moments of legal dispute, or at any other point. The suggestion is:

> All those who are born as or become citizens of India would come under the purview of this framework of common laws.... All citizens would also have the right to choose at any point in their lives to be governed by personal laws if they so desire. The choice to be governed by personal law has to be a conscious decision by an individual citizen. If such a choice is not made, the new gender just legislation would be applied. In keeping with our conceptual frame work of gender just laws as the rights of citizens, we believe that citizens, who have chosen personal laws should be able to revoke their choice and move back to the common laws at a moment of legal conflict (Working Group for Women's Rights 1996, 90–91).

The WGWR position marked a conceptual shift in the impasse between internal reform and common civil laws, staking a claim to women's rights by aiming at a comprehensive package of gender just laws, while acknowledging the pressures that women may face by allowing the option of choosing personal laws at any point. WGWR's efforts are not unlike that made by Shahnaz Shaikh in 1983 – that is, to make an unresponsive state respond to the oppression of minority women as citizens of the country – except that here, women (and men) are given the option of choosing personal law. Similarly, the AIDWA has suggested that work on the UCC or personal law reform be rejected in favour of expanding the pool of civil and criminal laws to provide women redressal from violence in areas that would not be seen as threatening, or alienating the minority communities. The focus is not only on personal laws, but includes other areas of law – domestic violence, criminal law, employment and labour laws – that are perhaps as misogynist as personal laws. As we will see in Chapter 4 and Chapter 6, on issues relating to women's sexuality and domestic violence, criminal and civil laws offer a continuum wherein the subordinate position of women is legitimised.

The sexualised female body in citizenship debates

There is a rich body of literature that looks at ways in which women's bodies are constructed as symbolically representing a community, nation or race (see for instance: Yuval-Davis and Anthias 1989; Kumari and De Alwis 1996). The representation of women's bodies can take different forms in peacetimes and conflict times. For instance, Indian women winning international beauty pageants in the 1990s have been seen as a source of national pride, symbolising the ways in which contemporary Indian women's bodies are now globally desirable and desired (Kishwar 1995, 26–31; Ahmed-Ghosh 2003, 205–22). This is a change from mainstream 'traditional' ways of controlling women's bodies through seclusion and sexual control.[15] While some have argued that this is a positive development, and allows women agency and control over the way their bodies are represented (Ghosh 1996, 150–183), others suggest that the consumerism and commodification of the female body works to fulfil male fantasies, and lead to an objectification of women's bodies (Kishwar 1995, 26–31). In addition to, and perhaps in contradiction to the sexualised image of the modern, globalised Indian woman is the image of the Indian woman as mother, her body recognised as serving a literal function as creating life and reproducing the nation, therefore the ideal woman's body is that of a mothers responsible for reproducing the ideal nation as in the case of 'Aryan' women in Nazi Germany (Koonz 1087). In peacetime therefore, and in periods of nation building therefore, the focus is on the bodies of women from one's own community, and there are efforts to control women's bodies so that they meet the national ideal. However, the body of the women constructed as the 'other': in this case, Muslim women and sex workers, are constructed as dangerous, and therefore marginalised. In this section we will look at how citizenship debates impact on and are impacted by sexualised images of women constructed as the 'other' to the normative Indian woman.

The sexualised Muslim woman: communal riots and Muslim women

In times of conflict, the focus shifts to the bodies of women from the enemy camp. Sexual violence against Muslim women and girls was a central plank of the Hindu fundamentalist agenda of the Sangh Parivar in communal riots from independence to the present (See: Butalia 1995; Jayawardena and De Alwis 1996; International

---

15   See Chapter 4 for more details on how sexual control can inhibit women's lives.

Initiative for Justice in Gujarat 2003). In 2002, anti-Muslim riots in the western state of Gujarat unleashed particularly horrific and violent forms of sexual violence against Muslim women that historian Tanika Sarkar sees as resulting from 'a dark sexual obsession about ultra-virile Muslim male bodies and overfertile Muslim female ones' (Sarkar, cited in Nussbaum 2004, 5).

I suggest that the 'sexual obsession' is based on pre-existing notions of Muslim male and female sexuality. As we have seen, MPL in India allows Muslim men to marry up to four times, which has been a matter of great concern to Hindu rightwing leaders, expressed not in terms of the rights of Muslim women, but expressed for Hindu men deprived of such 'privileges'. The more extreme right therefore expresses envy for the Muslim man's legal right to marry more than once. Swami Muktanand Saraswati, a member of the VHP stated, 'There are no (equal) laws regarding marriage. Today, a Hindu man can marry only one woman, while a Muslim man can have five wives. If a man wants to have 25 wives, let him' (Frontline 1993). Similarly, debates on the family planning policy in India have been concerned about rising population in the country, and sometimes included suggestions that Muslim populations in some parts of the country grow at a higher rate than other communities (Sahay 1996). Muslim women therefore are constructed as being sexually active, and fecund, therefore a threat to the mainstream Hindu notion of sexually controlled womanhood.

While Hindu men symbolically construct the bodies of Muslim women in India as being desirable and (normally) not accessible, the bodies of Muslim men are constructed as beastlike, rapacious and dangerous (to Hindu women). This has a resonance in other contexts, for instance, the construction of black men in white supremist discourse reveals a similar fear of the sexually aggressive and predatory black men (Jones 2004). Therefore in periods of war and conflict, women of the 'enemy' community, race or country are subjected to rape and torture, in order to get access to that which was unavailable in peacetimes. In addition, the rape is seen as a way to impregnate the enemy women in conflict situations (Jones 2004, 24–30). In Gujarat, rape accompanied torture and murder, and horrific incidents of raping, mutilating and murdering pregnant women have been interpreted as a form of genocide, by destroying future generations of Muslims (International Initiative for Justice in Gujarat 2003, 33).

In this context, rape is not a random act of male violence against women, but is an act committed to dishonour the woman and by extension her community, race or country. The 'dishonouring' however works only when the meaning of honour as symbolically vested primarily, in women's bodies is shared by both the communities of the perpetrators and the victims. Therefore, both perpetrators (Hindu fundamentalists) and victims (Muslims) have a shared understanding of sexual purity and impurity being vested in the bodies of women.[16] In the case of Gujarat, this has

---

16 It has been argued that notions of honour being vested in women's bodies is structurally a part of Hindu constructions of sexuality as in the Ramayana, where Lord Rama's rejection of Sita after her abduction by Ravana was based on his feelings of being dishonoured (Hess 1999, 5). See footnote 17 for more details on the Ramayana.

manifested itself in raped women being coerced or pressurised by the community to remain silent about their violation and abuse (International Initiative for Justice in Gujarat 2003, 74).

What has been significant about communal sexualised violence against Muslim women in the Gujarat riots is the complicity of some Hindu women in the violence. There have been documented cases of Hindu women encouraging men from their families and communities to attack Muslim men and women, and in some cases participate in the violence (International Initiative for Justice in Gujarat 2003, 33).

The issue of violent women, either within interpersonal or structural violence, is one that causes considerable discomfort to feminists. It can be argued that feminist debates in the west have concentrated essentially on male violence against women, therefore casting women in the role of perpetual victims of oppression (for instance, see articles in Yllo and Bograd 1998). Certainly addressing issues of how women complicit in patriarchy are rewarded for their actions can be difficult and painful for feminists.

However, we suggest that acknowledging these vexed issues does not necessarily lead to anti feminist repercussions. Rather as Indian feminists have recognised in the context of dowry related violence where mothers in law are often perpetrators of violence against daughters in law, understanding dynamics of women's violence against women can feed into an understanding of patriarchy (see Chapter 6). Therefore, women within patriarchies who accept contextually relevant patriarchal norms of female behaviour – sexual behaviour, dress, appearance, marital status, motherhood – are rewarded as long as they conform to these norms. However, most women are aware of the vulnerability of their acceptance, even as they enjoy the rewards of social approbation and esteem. For women therefore, punishing other women who threaten or transgress social norms or community cohesion can be a way of strengthening their position. Therefore the role of women as 'carriers of culture' (Yuval-Davis 1997) is reinforced when they oppress other women within their family or community. During times of conflict and war, including struggles for national liberation, there can be a necessary shift in women's role. In addition to reproducing the nation and the home, they are often called upon to demonstrate their loyalty by encouraging men to perpetuate violence against women and men from the 'enemy' camp or being violent themselves. Women encouraging men to sexual violence against 'enemy' women and physical violence against 'enemy' men enjoy power over the men and women of the 'other' community, while also enjoying praise and privileges for supporting national struggles.

Being a sex worker and being a citizen

As we will see in Chapter 4, legal debates on sex work aim to control and regulate women in the sex trade, rather than addressing violence within the trade or ways to redress it. Here I will look at the ways in which debates around trafficking for sex work construct sex workers as being primarily and conceptually 'outsiders' and non Indians, and therefore outside the realm of citizenship debates.

Women in sex work have been portrayed as transgressing moral parameters of acceptable gender behaviour. In 1986, the law governing prostitution and trafficking was amended, leading to a change in the name of the law from Suppression of Immoral Traffic in Women to Immoral Traffic abbreviated to SITA to the proposed Immoral Traffic in Women and Children (Prevention) Act abbreviated to PITA. This move was met with relief by some MPs, not because the amendments led to improvements in law, but because SITA was the name of a respected Hindu goddess, represented within mainstream Hindu tradition as the ideal wife:

> Another feature of the bill is that the nomenclature ... which was very ridiculous has been changed. The Suppression of Immoral Traffic Act, which was popularly known as SITA has been changed. I remember in courts of law so many hundreds of Sitas used to stand and we used to refer to them as Sita No. 1, Sita No. 2 and Sita no. 3. It is very rightful that this name has been changed (Shri Shantaram Naik, Lok Sabha Debates 1986b, 158).

There is clearly an elision between Sita, the ideal Hindu wife and Indian womanhood, contrasted with, in these debates with the image of the prostitute, and to call the latter, Sita causes anguish and discomfort. The popularity of the 'Sita' image of ideal wifehood has been the focus of immense debate, with Sita being seen by a Muslim Supreme Court judge as 'the noblest flower of Indian womanhood, devoted to her lord in thought, word and deed'[17] (Justice Hidayatullah cited in Hess 1999, 2).

Under PITA, the powers of the police to prevent trafficking were expanded, empowering trafficking police officers accompanying Special Police Officer to search any premises without a warrant. Other than PITA, trafficking for prostitution is subjected to other legal provisions other than PITA, including Section 366A IPC which prohibits procurement of minor girls for 'illicit intercourse; Section 366 B which prohibits importing minors from another country for the purpose of prostitution. Selling and buying of minors for the purpose of prostitution is also proscribed under Section 372 and 373. In addition to these provisions, women in prostitution are subjected to provisions in the Police Acts that aim to control 'indecent behaviour' and 'public nuisance', and can be arrested under Section 292 IPC for obscenity.

The laws against publicly visible prostitution reveal a deep discomfort with 'uncontrolled' sexuality, i.e., sexuality that is not confined to the private – and controllable domain. An adult woman found guilty of prostitution can be therefore be arrested for indecent exposure or soliciting under three different laws: PITA, the Indian Penal Code, and relevant Police Acts. In addition the Prevention of Pushing and Forcing a Girl Child into the Flesh Trade and Immoral Traffic Bill, discussed

---

17 Sita's story is a part of the hindu epic, Ramayana. She was the consort of Lord Rama, prince of Ayodhya, and she underwent a number of trials and tribulations, including following her husband in a nomadic and penurious life when he was unjustly exiled for 14 years; being abducted by Ravana, king of Sri Lanka; being rescued by Rama, but then forced to go through a 'trial by fire' (agni pariksa) to prove her chastity; and then abandoned by him when she was pregnant, and being asked to prove her faithfulness by Rama several years later; at which point, she asked for Mother Earth to swallow her as a sign of her virtue.

in the Indian Parliament, and at the time of writing (2006), awaiting tabling before the Lok Sabha is aimed at preventing specifically the entry of "girl children" defined as women under the age of 18, into the sex trade. Section 4 of the Act states that the punishment for a "person pushing or forcing a girl child into the flesh trade" is the death penalty, and a client of a girl child in the flesh trade can be punished by life imprisonment (Prevention of Pushing and Forcing a Girl Child into the Flesh Trade and Immoral Traffic Act, 2005). Therefore "trafficking" of young women constructed legally as "girl children" is seen as a serious criminal offence; while the trade itself is designated as "flesh trade" and "immoral" traffic.

While anti trafficking laws construct the sex trade, and by extension sex workers as being immoral and therefore the 'other' of the virtuous Hindu wife, constructing the sex worker as 'foreign' is another way in which national discourse on sex work avoids the reality of Indian women working as sex workers.[18] Much debate in India focuses on the trafficking of women from neighbouring countries including Nepal and Bangladesh for the purposes of trafficking, which is reflected in international agreements on trafficking to which India is a signatory. For instance, the Convention on Combating the Crimes of Trafficking in Women and Children, was created and debated in the ninth SAARC[19] Summit held in Maldives, where SAARC nations declared their concern and readiness to combat trafficking of women and children, and to create and strengthen national laws against trafficking for sex work. The SAARC Convention associates trafficking and prostitution with loss of dignity and a violation of human rights. Trafficking is defined in essentially homogenised ways that does not take into cognisance the consent of the person trafficked. To quote:

> Trafficking means the moving, selling or buying of women and children (for prostitution) within and outside a country for monetary or other considerations with or without the consent of the person subjected to trafficking (SAARC 1998, 27th Paragraph).

The absence of the concept of consent for adult women denies any notion of agency or self-determination. The Convention defines 'prostitution' as the sexual exploitation or abuse of persons for commercial purposes, and makes it compulsory for member States to criminalise trafficking. However, the definition of trafficking in this convention does not include other experienced of trafficked women, men and children, including forced entry into sites such as marriage, bonded labour, camel jockeying and the organ trade. Some feminists have suggested that trafficking and prostitution need to be separated, as trafficking is one of the possible ways in which women and children can enter prostitution, and prostitution is only one of the sites to which women; men and children are trafficked. Trafficking is the entry point, while

---

18   Elsewhere I have argued that in reality trans national trafficking is only one of the ways in which women enter sex work, and that intra country migration often forms the basis of women's entry into the sex trade. See Gangoli, G. (2001).

19   SAARC stands for South Asian Association for Regional Cooperation; members states are: Nepal, India, Pakistan, Bangladesh and Sri Lanka.

prostitution is the site to which women and children are trafficked (South Asian Women's Groups 1998, 44).

Since the SAARC Convention defines trafficking so narrowly on the one hand, as entry into prostitution; and so broadly on the other, as entry whether voluntary or coercive into prostitution; member states including India are faced with confusing legal choices, with human rights implications. Therefore, the SAARC Convention directs member states to criminalise living off the earnings of prostitution, which criminalises children and other family members who are financially dependent on the income of sex workers. It also places responsibility is placed on the country of origin in the case of repatriation and rehabilitation of sex workers from another country (SAARC 1998, 27th Paragraph). No guidelines are set for the modalities of repatriation. Nor is any responsibility placed on the country of residence to protect women and children from violence.

This has implications for women in prostitution who are repatriated between countries in South Asia due to their status as prostitutes, leading to violence and rights violations. A report on the 'rescue' of commercial sex workers from red light areas in Bombay in 1995 brings out some of the lacunae in existing procedure. The report states:

> ...it appears that the manner in which these raids is being conducted is neither meeting the stated goals of the High Court in preventing the spread of disease, as the traffickers can easily replace the detained girls with fresh ones, nor is (there a) rehabilitation plan, nor is it consistent with the goals of the Convention on the Rights of the Child, for the same reason and also because the preventive aspects are continuing to be ignored, such as the arrest of traffickers, additionally, we feel that the rights of the detained girls are being violated since they are being held against their will without being offered as rehabilitation plan and in institutions, both Government and private, that had not been given any time or choice about making any plans for them. Thus the current conditions in which many of them are residing are in some important ways worse than that they experience in the brothels (Fernandes, G. and C. Stewart-Ray nd, 99)).

Concern has been expressed that the Convention can become an instrument to curb women's mobility from one country to another within the SAARC region. This is not a completely irrelevant fear, as unaccompanied women from Nepal travelling across the Indo-Nepal border have been prevented entry into India, even if there is no evidence of trafficking, or that they plan to enter prostitution (South Asian Women's Group 1998).

This seems puzzling at first glance, since this would not legally be understood as trafficking, because by its very definition, trafficking involves the presence of other people, other than the person trafficked. Hence, isolating and preventing single or unaccompanied women from travelling seems a puzzling policy, unless one considers that it is done to monitor the migration and movement of women, who are considered a sexual threat, in this case single and unaccompanied women.

Feminists have pointed to the need for international conventions to emphasise the voluntary return of women to the country of origin, and to ensure that trafficked persons are not subjected to discriminatory treatment in law or practice (Wijer and Lin 1997). However, countries in South Asia often disagree with each other on the responsibilities of each state regarding women in sex work. At the World Congress against Commercial Sexual Exploitation of Children, Stockholm in August 1996, there were moments of tension between Indian and Nepali NGOs and officials, following the repatriation of Nepalise sex workers from Nepal from Bombay. A representative of a Nepali NGO working with repatriated women in prostitution stated that:

> These Nepalis are victims of very well organised trafficking networks. They don't know and neither do their parents that they are being sent to work as prostitutes in India... If India really wanted to do something about the problem, it can (cited in Sinha 1996, 3).

She added that Nepali women infected with HIV were being sent back after such raids and added to the threat of AIDS in the country, and stated that there were no brothels in Nepal, 'but this trade means that this country is being unnecessarily exposed to all this' (cited in Sinha 1996, 3). A possible reason for this perception is that the first AIDS case recorded in Nepal was discovered in 1986 among Nepali women who had returned from brothels in India (HRW 1995). The Nepali perception is that Nepali women and girls are coerced into prostitution without the knowledge or consent of their families and that their return to Nepal caused social tensions and upheaval. The Indian NGO response is that the Nepalis civil society should share responsibility for this situation. It is essentially a discourse in which women and girls in prostitution are not given agency, even by activists in the field, but are seen either as victims – when they leave the country, or as harbingers of doom – when they re-enter.

Trafficking therefore, is an area where citizenship debates are centred. Nowhere is this clearer than in the following statement by Vijay Bhaskar, Secretary, Department of Women and Child Development, Human Resource Ministry.

> Repatriation of (immigrant) prostitutes is a basic citizenship issue. Non-citizens can't stay in the country without valid papers. If we accept nation states, we can't help repatriating them.[20]

However, repatriation is also an issue of human rights, further complicated when one recognises that the diplomatic relations between South Asian countries vary. For example, India and Nepal have an open border and citizens from both countries have the right to travel to and reside in the other country (HRW 1995). Hence, preventing women from travelling between Nepal and India violates this treaty, especially when they are being preventing on the basis of suspicion of being prostitutes, and of intending to enter prostitution.

Issues around citizenship and sex work have also been raised in the context of debates on the ban on 'bar dancers' in the city of Mumbai were centred around claims

---

20   Interviewed on 3 September 1998.

by the ruling party that some dancers were 'illegal' and trafficked Bang
opposed by feminists who focussed on the 'Indian' status of most of the bar
Indeed a union formed by bar dancers in 2005 after intense discussions wa:
'Bhartiya Bar Girls Union' (Union of Indian Bar Girls) precisely to counter these
'accusations' on being non citizens (RCWS and FAOW 2005, 5). While some
feminists involved in this issue have noted their discomfort with having to articulate
their demands in this manner, they suggest that there is a certain inevitability when
the rights and livelihoods of the majority of women in concerned.

Limitations of citizenship debates

While some feminists have appealed to the Indian State on the basis of equal rights
as citizens, we have seen that this restricts the debates to women deemed as 'true'
citizens therefore leaving out non citizens (sex workers from another country), or
shadow citizens whose citizenship while guaranteed in the constitution is nevertheless
contested at a day to day level (minority Muslim women). As the bar dancers ban
debates bring out feminists who may otherwise believe in the rights of all women
irrespective of their legal status, are forced to enter into debates and counter claims of
who is a citizen, and therefore eligible for protection, and who by extension, is not.

Simultaneously, there are concerns expressed within the women's movement
appeals by concerned groups – including feminists – to the state to reform, change or
introduce laws recognises and validates the superior status of the state over citizens,
therefore further legitimising the state. Therefore some feminists suggest that a move
be made to non legalist appeals, and work within community and caste groups on
women's rights, that are culturally contextual, and not defined by or indeed limited
by rhetoric of nationalist debates, or debates on citizenship.[21] Others, however argue
in favour of multiple strategies, including legal reform based on citizen rights, where
appropriate, and human or women's rights, where the latter are too restrictive.

---

21 Madhu Bhushan, activist, Vimochana, during a meeting on Gender Just Laws in
Bombay. 1–4 December 1995. Organised by Forum Against Oppression of Women.

Chapter 4

The Legal Regulation of Women's Sexuality: Continuum between Civil and Criminal Laws

This chapter will trace the varied ways in which criminal and civil laws in India construct women's sexuality as subordinate to male sexuality and systematise sexuality within a marital, heterosexist paradigm. A range of criminal and civil laws will be analysed from this perspective, including laws on rape, prostitution, maintenance, adultery, divorce, homosexuality and pornography, and we will assess whether there is a continuum between criminal and civil law as far as the construction of women's sexuality is concerned. Further, the chapter will access how Indian feminists have conceptualised sexuality. We will examine the view that the focus on legal rights and campaigns to amend the anomalies of law has created a narrow and rigid view of sexuality within Indian feminism, wherein sexuality became an adjunct to discussions on rape, adultery, rape and personal laws, but was rarely seen as the flowering of women's identity (Dietrich 1992, 3). Some issues relating to sexuality have therefore been unexamined within Indian feminist movements, leading to a meaningful silence on some aspects. These include: feminist understanding of morality, marriage, monogamy and socially coercive heterosexuality. Sex workers organisations and gay rights groups have argued that feminists have not consistently taken a stand on debates on prostitution or gay rights. One of the issues we will be looking at in this chapter is the validity of these claims; whether the silence is linked to Indian feminists wanting to disengage themselves from debates that may be seen as 'western' orientated, thus producing a strategic silence, or is it due to the cultural problems of discussing sex and sexuality within India and the ways in which feminists have responded to these challenges. The chapter will first focus on legal interpretations of women's sexuality in laws relating to sexual control of women within marriage; to sexual assault and sexual harassment; to sexual practices constructed as 'unnatural' therefore homosexuality or deviant, such as prostitution and pornography and finally on feminist responses to issues of sexuality.

Sexual control within marriage

As we will see in this section civil and criminal laws in India collude to control women's sexuality within marriage.

Rape within marriage

The rape law is based on, and legitimises several patriarchal presumptions, and attitudes regarding male and female sexuality.[1] While purporting to provide justice to raped women, the laws in actuality reinforce patterns of heterosexual dominance in which women are seen as inferior, sexually passive and within marriage, the sexual property of their husbands. The rape law defines the offence in terms of penile penetration into the vagina, therefore legitimizing male notions of what constitutes sex. In addition, the rape law sanctions sexual abuse of women within marriage by not recognising marital rape as a legal category under Section 375 IPC. The law does offer protection from marital rape for judicially separated married women, however this clause is nullified by the provisions in another law, that is restitution of conjugal rights under Hindu Marriage Act, 1955. Under this provision, if one spouse files for restitution of conjugal rights, the court can direct the absconding spouse to reside with the petitioner (HMA 1955, Section 9). This provision colludes with, if not actively validates marital rape.

Decrees of restitution of conjugal rights have been granted by judges on the grounds of the duty of a Hindu wife to live with her husband. In one case decided by the High Court in Punjab, the wife's employment in a school caused her to reside in a separate location from her husband. She was unwilling to resign her job and join her husband at his instance. The husband applied for restitution of conjugal rights under Section 9, HMA. The wife pleaded that she wanted the marriage to continue, and was willing to visit her husband, and to allow him to visit her occasionally. The judge refused to dismiss the restitution plea, and held forth on the duties of a Hindu wife:

> Under the Hindu law, a wife's duty to her husband is to submit herself obediently to his authority, and to remain under his roof and protection. She is not, therefore, entitled to separate residence and maintenance, unless she proves that by reason of his misconduct, or by his refusal to maintain her in his own place of residence, or for any justifying clause, she is compelled to stay away. It is not possible to accede to the contention that because the wife's work compels her to live away, and she is not willing to resign her job, the husband should content himself by visiting his wife whenever he wishes to live with her, or co-habit with her, or by her coming to live with him occasionally (Smt. Tirath Kaur v. Kirpal Singh 1964, 28).

The wife's career and work outside the house, and her refusal to resign her job is constructed as an act of rebellion that must be crushed by injunctions of wifely obedience. Refusal to live with the husband is justified only in cases of violence, or

---

1   Chapter 5 will analyse the feminist campaigns in India in the 1980s that led to the amendment of the rape law in 1983, creating a new category of 'custodial rape' and the implications of this amendment. Here, we will examine the ways in which debates around rape (feminist and state) feed into, and conflict with norms of female and male sexual behaviour, both within marriage and outside it.

the refusal of the husband to maintain the wife. The judgment negates the assertion of a woman's economic independence, and simultaneously rejects any redefinition of marriage where the husband does not have unlimited sexual access over his wife.

That the clause on restitution of conjugal rights legitimises marital rape was recognised in a 1983 judgment of the Andhra Pradesh High Court (T Sareetha v. T Venkatasubbaih 1983, 356). T Sareetha was a well known actress in Andhra Pradesh. Following physical violence, Sareetha was staying away from her husband, T Venkatasubbaih. Her husband, who was financially dependent on Sareetha, filed for restitution of conjugal rights. On the face of it, the judgment appears to be influenced by feminist language, as the Judge declared Section 9, HMA, 1955 to be unconstitutional.

....a court decree enforcing restitution of conjugal rights constitutes the starkest form of government invasion of personal identity, and the individual's zone of intimate decisions. The victim is stripped of its control over the various parts of its body subjected to the humiliating sexual molestation accompanied by a forcible loss of the precious right to decide when, if at all her body should be allowed to give birth to another human being... Above all, the decree of restitution of conjugal rights makes the unwilling victim's body a soulless and joyless vehicle for bringing into existence another human being...Pregnancy would be foisted on her by the state.... Such a law violates the right to privacy and human dignity guaranteed by, and contained in Article 21 of our constitution (T Sareetha v. T Venkatasubbaih 1983, 356).

While the judgement has been seen as positively upholding married women's rights over their body, Sections of the Indian Women's Movement (IWM) welcomed the judgment. However, significant as this judgment was, one can read another kind of objectification into it. The woman is described as a victim; the pronoun used for her is 'it', thereby objectifying her. Nor is the experience named as rape, but is called 'humiliating sexual molestation', which is seen as most violative of the woman's rights if it results in unwanted pregnancy. Therefore, as in the rape law, penetrative sex becomes the defining criterion, with its emphasis on potential impregnation of the woman. While the judgment attempted in theory to bury the concept that the wife is the legal property of the husband, it does not address concerns that women have used the restitution decree in case of desertion. Therefore it was not entirely against women's interests (Gandhi and Shah 1992, 231–2).This judgment was overturned by a Supreme Court judgment in 1984, based on the understanding that the restitution decree merely enjoins cohabitation, and not sexual relations between the spouses, therefore declining to hold Section 9, Hindu Marriage Act, 1955 as invalid (Saroj Rani v. Sudarshan Kumar Chadda 1984, 1562).

Marital rape is also condoned in other civil laws relating to marriage and divorce. In one case filed under Indian Divorce Act (section 18 and 19 (i)), applicable to Christians, the husband filed for divorce on the grounds that the wife was impotent, as she had refused to consent to sexual intercourse immediately after the marriage. The Bombay High Court judgment supported his claim, stating that:

All efforts on the part of the appellant by way of endearment was thwarted by the respondent stating that it was too early to indulge in any sexual acts. The appellant has gone so far as to say, "In any event, the respondent submitted herself most reluctantly and she was only a passive factor on the first night." (Vincent Adolf Gondinho v. June Beatrice Rana Gondinho 1984, 930).

The judgment focused on the evidence of the man that on that single occasion of sexual intimacy, he was 'unable to penetrate her':

> The question that arises is, can a woman who submits only on one occasion to sexual intercourse with her husband, and that too only by the husband using force, and resists successfully the attempts of the husband to have sexual relations with her be said to be impotent relative to her? In our opinion, the answer to that question should be in the affirmative...We set aside the order passed by the trial judge and pronounce a decree for nullity of marriage in favour of the appellant and against the respondent (Vincent Adolf Gondinho v. June Beatrice Rana Gondinho 1984, 930).

Sexual control within marriage

As we have seen in the preceding section, marital rape is legitimised and condoned in criminal and civil law, which legitimises social norms of male superiority within marriage. This is strengthened in other clauses of marriage laws. For instance, civil marriage laws have differential minimum age of marriage for women and men (18 years for women and 21 for men), which confirms the socially maintained hierarchy of age and experience. The mainstream Hindu cultural expectation in marriage is that of male hypogamy and female hypergamy, therefore men are expected to be older, have social experience, maturity, and hence can be dominant in relation to their wives. The law also reflects the social and cultural concern for confining the sexuality of young women within marriage as soon as she attains sexual maturity (Fruzetti 1982, 4–5). Sexual control of husbands over wives is similarly emphasised in the adultery law (Section 497 IPC), which is a part of the criminal law.[2] According to Section 497 IPC:

> Whoever has sexual intercourse with a person who is, and whom he knows or has reason to believe to be the wife of another man, without the consent or connivance of that man, such sexual intercourse not amounting to the offence of rape is guilty of the offence of adultery (Section 497 IPC).

Section 497 therefore punishes the man who has a sexual relationship with a married woman, not a woman who has a sexual relation outside marriage. A 1985 Supreme Court judgment explicated the logic of the act:

> The law only makes a specific kind of extra marital relationship an offence...the relationship between a man and a married woman...the legislature is entitled to deal with

---

2   Adultery is also a ground for divorce under the different marriage laws. Under the criminal law, Section 497 IPC, it is however punishable by imprisonment.

the evil where it is felt and seen the most, (that is in the case of) a man seducing the wife of another (Soumitra Vishnu v. Union of India 1985, 1618).

Feminists have argued that the adultery law is a throwback to Brahmanical patriarchy, because in the Hindu scriptures, the very word for adultery is 'connection with another man's wife' (Abraham 1987,16–20), rather than general understanding of the word as meaning lack of sexual fidelity with one's own spouse or another's, or lack of chastity. Dubious as all the meanings of the word are, the one chosen in Section 497 IPC entrenches male control over women. The inferences that we can draw from this law are twofold. One that the man owns his wife sexually, and his consent is necessary to gain sexual access over her. Second, the offence of adultery is legally equivalent to that of theft, the goods being the wife's body. Women are therefore denied agency, whether they themselves have committed adultery (as understood generally) or are married to men committing adultery.

Where laws recognise women's sexual agency within marriage, it is constructed as being dangerous. Maintenance and custody laws under different civil and criminal provisions provide for the rescinding of maintenance order or loss of custody of children if the woman can be proven to be 'unchaste'(HMA 1955, Section 25 (3); SMA 1954, Section37 (3); Parsee Marriage and Divorce Act 1937, Section 40 (3); Hindu Adoption and Maintenance Act 1956, Section 18 (3); Section 125 (5) CrPC).

While the varied legal provisions on maintenance have been described as 'a confusing maze of laws based on religion' (Agnes 1992, 26), there is a discernible pattern in the maze. Under all the laws, the divorced or separated wife is entitled to maintenance only if she is sexually inaccessible to any man other than the husband, and is described in terms of chastity and sexual morality. While some civil laws allow husbands to apply for maintenance and such men engaging in sexual activity with women are similarly penalised, the language used in the laws to describe the 'aberration' is not loaded with moralistic nuances, and the relevant laws baldly state that, 'if such party is the husband, that he had sexual intercourse with any woman outside the marriage' (Hindu Marriage Act 1955, Section 25 (3); Parsee Marriage and Divorce Act 1937, Section 40 (3)). Therefore it appears that married women's sexual 'transgressions' are read legally as absence of chastity, while in the case of men, it is reduced to a 'factual ' description of a specific sexual act.

Under maintenance laws, fidelity and chastity for women is equated not only with sexual abstinence after separation or divorce, but also with a number of other provisions. Under Section 125 CrPC, a woman who 'refuses to live with her husband without sufficient reason' is similarly denied maintenance, while under the HMA, a divorce on the grounds of mutual consent is another ground for refusing maintenance (Hindu Marriage Act 1955, Section 25 (3); Section 125 (5) CrPC). Therefore maintenance laws are only available to women who do not breach normative wifely expectations prior to, and after separation or divorce.

In general, within the judicial system, divorced and separated women are treated with ambivalence, reflecting social norms that veer between pity and horror at the fate of such women. In a 1986 case on maintenance, the Jaipur High Court judge raised the maintenance amount fixed by the Sessions Court from Rs. 200 to Rs. 350 a month. The husband was a lecturer in a college, and during a marital dispute, the wife burnt his thesis. The husband filed for and was awarded a divorce on the grounds of cruelty. The woman then filed for increasing the maintenance amount in the Rajasthan High Court. The judge held that, '...a divorced wife (sic) is a cursed human being, abhorred by society', and that in her case, 'remarriage ...is a very difficult and far fetched provision', therefore increasing the maintenance amount set in lower courts (Smt. Shanta Devi v. Raghav Prakash 1986, 13).

In another case, also heard by the Bombay High Court, a policeman was directed to pay his wife a monthly maintenance of Rs. 300. Two months after the decree, he sent her a divorce decree under Muslim law, and stated that he was not entitled to pay her anything under the Muslim Women (Right to Protection on Divorce) act, 1986. When the woman filed for her arrears, the judge humiliated her by throwing her papers at her. The husband accused her in the courtroom of being 'immoral', and she was laughed at by the court clerks in the presence of the judge (Agnes 1992, 130).

The ridicule and humiliation that some women routinely face in the court room in maintenance cases acts as a deterrent to other women from transgressing social and sexual norms, thereby fixes women who are sexually active outside marriage or take independent decisions regarding their lives as 'bad' woman, open to, and deserving of, ill treatment at the hands of their families and the authorities. These laws and judicial practices therefore serve to legitimise subordination of women within the family and are based on ideas of marriage and heterosexuality as normative. We will now look at how non-marital sexuality is constructed in law.

Rape and sexual morality

In cases of rape as in maintenance cases, judicial pronouncements governed by extra legal considerations of morality, virtuousness and appropriate sexual behavior, seem to favour men. Within marriage, the appropriate sexual behavior for married women is understood to be sexually accessible to their husbands, while to be treated favourably in rape cases, single women have to conform to sexual norms by appearing virginal and 'innocent'. In one case involving the abduction and gang rape of a minor, the judge called the rape 'a bestial act of lust', suggestion that the young woman's failure to report the case immediately after the event could be understood in terms of the 'inherent bashfulness, the innocent naiveté and the feminine tendency to conceal the outrage of masculine aggression are factors that led to concealment by the girl' (Krishnalal v. State of Haryana 1980, 1252). The paternalistic concern for the young woman's loss of virginity veils other concerns. The judgment does not question the use of sexual power by the three men, but sees it as a crime of passion. The reasoning in the judgment closely follows that of the 1980 Law Commission on the rape law, which expressed the view that '...a person out to commit rape is motivated by a strong, uncontrollable passion or the lust of a savage' (Government of India 1980, 8).

The understanding that rape is a crime of passion, rather than an expression of male violence against women, allows courts to treat perpetrators in rape cases with leniency. In a case involving a 22-year-old man who raped his 24-year-old cousin, the apex court reduced the sentence of his offender, on the grounds that he was very young, was 'overcome by sex stress' and the victim was 'temptingly lonely' (AIR 1980, 249), therefore reconceptualising an act of violence into a sexual odyssey, while the description of the woman as 'temptingly lonely' objectifies her, holding her at least partly responsible for the rape. The sentence was thereby reduced, and the judgement converted the offender to a victim of circumstances and of social permissiveness:

> It may be marginally extenuating to mention that modern Indian conditions are drifting into societal permissiveness on the carnal front, prompting proneness to pornos (sic) in real life, what with libidinous "brahmacharis", womanising public men, lascivious dating and mating by unwed students. Isolated prosecutions and annual suppression rhetoric will stultify the law, where the vice is widespread and the larger felons are left loose (AIR 1980, 249).

The suggestion that generalised sexual 'permissiveness' contributes to rape therefore brings legal rhetoric in to the realm of normative notions of sexual behaviour, where no distinction is made between consensual sexual activity, and violent and coercive sex.

Sexual harassment

Sexual harassment of women is an endemic part of public life in India (Baxi 2001), and can be understood as an expression of masculine sexual control over women who have stepped out of the normative private sphere. Sexual harassment of women in public places is named and culturally constructed in India as 'eve teasing', a specifically 'Indian-English' term. The semantic roots of the term, 'eves' as temptresses being 'teased' normalises and trivialises the issue.

While there are specific laws that can be used in cases of sexual harassment, most of them have been recognised as being inadequate, and based on outdated notions of women's propriety. For instance, Section 509 IPC criminalises any 'word, gesture or act intended to insult the modesty of a woman' and Section 354 IPC criminalises 'assault or criminal force to a woman with the intention to outrage her modesty'. In addition, Section 209, IPC criminalises 'obscene acts and songs'. These provisions of the IPC date back to the nineteenth century, and feminists have argued that they are wholly inadequate in defining the experiences of women (Agnes 1992, 19–33). Further, while 'eve teasing' is a social construction that devalues women's experiences and is not a legal offence, it is accepted and interpreted by the police as valid in naming and understanding cases of sexual assault. Therefore in the 1994 Crimes Against Women Report, Section 354 is named 'Molestation/Eve teasing' (cited in Baxi 2001), pointing to the slippages between the categories of eve teasing, outraging women's modesty and sexual harassment in official discourses.

The Indian women's movement campaigned on sexual harassment of women in the workplace through the 1980s and 1990s (Chakravarti and Wahi 1995), the first feminist challenge to the paucity of legal provisions on sexual harassment was made in 1997, when a Public Interest Litigation (PIL) was filed by women's organizations in the Supreme Court of India, following the gang rape by 5 members of the same caste of Bhanwari Devi, an employee of the Rajasthan State sponsored Women's Development Programme (WDP) as a reprisal for her efforts to stop child marriage primarily among upper-caste Gujjars and Brahmins (see Gangoli 1998b, 128–136). The Sessions Court judgement on the rape case rejected Bhanwari Devi's claims that she had been raped,[3] leading to sections of Indian feminists feeling outraged and disappointed. While some feminists saw in the judgement a vindication of their position that the legal system, given its inherently patriarchal nature, could not give justice to women, others decided to use the Bhanwari Devi case to get rights for all women in cases of sexual harassment and assault taking place within the workplace situation, thus resulting in the PIL.

The Supreme Court judgement responding to the PIL addressed the issue of sexual harassment in the workplace in terms of violation of Fundamental Rights in the Indian constitution, and international conventions on gender equality that India was a signatory to, suggesting that absence of adequate civil and penal laws made it necessary for the court to create guidelines to ensure prevention of sexual harassment of women (Vishakha and Anrs. v. Union of India 1997, 3011). The judgement therefore was a part of a general trend of judicial activism in the 1990s, wherein judges were pointing to gaps in existing law, and using their powers to address these, thereby belying the view that the legal system was inherently patriarchal. The guidelines placed the responsibility of preventing and addressing cases of sexual harassment in the workplace on employers, including setting up complaint mechanisms and complaint committees. The seriousness with which the Supreme Court judgement was taken is evident in the creation of a law on sexual harassment, passed in 2003 (Sexual harassment of women in their Workplace (Prevention) Bill, 2003).

The judgement and the law shift the 'blame' and 'responsibility' of the incidents of sexual harassment from the individuals involved to the employer. While potentially useful for women experiencing sexual harassment, however, it is argued that the law does not go far enough in defining sexual harassment as 'including avoidable sexual advances', while the judgement provides a wider definition of sexual harassment as including 'unwelcome sexually determined behavior', which forefronts women's articulations in defining male actions as harassment. The law is not generally or widely applicable, leaves out of its scope, some 'workplace' locations, including 'free trade zones, special economic zones, multinational companies, offices/firms of professionals such as lawyers, doctors, chartered accountants, teachers, and many others such as religious bodies and institutes' (Raymond 2003).

These limitations point to the complexities in creating a law that is entirely comprehensive, or inclusive of all potential experiences that women have in the

---

3   See Chapter 5 for more details on the judgement.

workplace. At another level, the laws on sexual harassment can be conceptualised as casting women as victims that need protection at all times, in all locations, which could lead to employers expressing reluctance to employ women, due to the need for providing extra protection. This can be compared with trade union and employers' response to other legally enforceable provisions such as maternity benefits, provision of crèches etc, which are used as excuses to not employ women employees of childbearing ages, or to remove from employment young women who are seen as most likely to use these provisions (Gangoli 1992).[4] Feminists have therefore the difficult task of convincing trade unions and employers that women employers are not an employment liability, while arguing that they have rights as employees.

Deviant sexualities and the law

This section will look at the ways in which the law understands and deals with what are conceptualised as deviant sexual practices: homosexuality, prostitution and pornography, and the implications for women and men.

'Against the order of nature': homosexuality and the law

The law has defined normalcy of sexual behavior with heterosexuality as the defining factor. Section 377, IPC, introduced in 1860, under colonial rule states that:

> Whoever voluntarily has carnal intercourse against the order of nature with any man, woman or animal shall be punished with (imprisonment of life), or with imprisonment of either description for a term which may extend to 10 years and shall be liable to fine.

> Explanation– Penetration is sufficient to constitute the carnal intercourse necessary for the offence described in this section (Section 377 IPC)

Section 377 IPC criminalises sodomy, not homosexuality per se. Legally, a person cannot be punished under this provision for being homosexual, but for performing the act of sodomy, therefore reflects the judicial attitude that sodomy is one of the most reprehensible form that sexual activity can take. The law therefore applies only in cases of male homosexual activity, not for lesbian sexual activity.

While the law seems to work to women's advantage, it has been argued that the act does not encourage or even condone lesbianism. It has been designed in this way because the very notion of women relating to women sexually is so offensive that it is not even taken cognizance of. Besides, the cultural construction of sexuality negates any sexual activity that is 'non productive' of male semen. On the other hand, it penalises homosexual men for the loss of the semen, which holds the 'seed' for reproduction (Aids Bhedbhav Virodhi Andolan 1991, 29). The disrepute of male

---

4   Interview with Sujata Ghatoskar, activist with Blue Star Trade Union on 25 March 2001.

homosexuality in law owes to the low status that women have in society. According to this argument, men view themselves, and are viewed as subjects, as authentic persons, and women, their sexual intimates are objects. For a man to relate to another man sexually means that he must 'reduce' himself to the level of a woman, by become an object for another man. This is seen as abhorrent and inappropriate.[5]

While the enforcement rate for Section 377 is extremely low, the act is used by the police to terrorise and blackmail gay men.[6] The legal notion of privacy held sacred when it comes to marriage is discarded when it comes to consensual homosexuality, and to sodomy within marriage.[7]

Gay rights groups have worked to influence the Indian state to withdraw Section 377 IPC by legal means and lobbying the state. The legal means include a petition filed in the Delhi High Court in 2001 against the act by members of an NGO working on HIV-AIDS prevention on the grounds that they could not work effectively to propagate safe sex practices in the gay community due to the law, and that the police were using the law to harass members of the gay communities. The petition was dismissed and the court ruled that the law could not be challenged by anyone 'not affected by it'(Human Rights Watch 2004).

Given that practicing homosexuality is illegal, it would potentially be difficult those most affected by it to challenge, therefore the judgement was possibly an effort to silence opposition to the law. What is interesting about this petition, and the connected protests is that lesbian women from feminist organizations, who are not directly affected by the law, have been consistently active in fighting it. This is partly due to Indian feminists' links with other social movements and, but also due to a recognition borne out in the late twentieth century that lesbianism in India is only tolerated when it is silent, and invisibilised. For lesbian – and non lesbian – feminists to come out and protest against an unjust law on (male) homosexuality is therefore a way of raising the profile of the issue within Indian society.

---

5   Interview with Bombay based gay rights activist on 29 September 2000, name withheld on request.

6   Study conducted by Independent Research Board on Law Reports. 1990 reveals the following figures:

	No. of cases	No. of convictions	Consent	Non consent
1970–79	5	3	–	–
1980–89	2	2	1	1

7   Under the Hindu Marriage Act, 1955, sodomy and bestiality are grounds for divorce. But if the woman is a consenting partner, it means that she, along with her husband, is held guilty under Section 377.

Immoral women or victims: laws on prostitution

Prostitution in India is, at the time of writing regulated through the Immoral Traffic in Women and Girls (Prevention) Act, 1986 (PITA).[8] As we have seen in the previous chapter, PITA displays ambivalence towards prostitution, as it is neither formulated to give justice to practitioners, nor to eradicate prostitution.

Under PITA, prostitution is not an illegal activity, however activities associated with prostitution such as brothel keeping and soliciting in public places is criminalised. In reality, it makes the practice of prostitution difficult, though not impossible (de Cunha 1991, 43–45). PITA displays the official and social concern of looking at prostitution as a safety valve, male sexuality being seen as uncontrolled, and uncontrollable. There seems a continuum in the attitudes displayed in the following official statement by the Government of India in the late nineteenth-century, and the excerpt from an interview with a police inspector working in a red light area in Bombay. The statement by an official in the British army in the late nineteenth century reads:

> The absence of prostitutes in cantonments where large numbers of young, unmarried soldiers are living would probably lead to offences such as criminal assault, rape and unnatural crime (cited in Ballhatchet 1980, 79).

The following excerpt from an interview with a police inspector in Kamathipura in 1995 echoes this sentiment:

> According to me, prostitutes are social workers – if it was not for them, women from good families would not be able to walk on the streets of Bombay. Men would attack women to get rid of their lustful impulses. [9]

As we have seen interpretations of the rape law have relied on similar social constructions of men possessing uncontrollable sexual urges. Some activists have used these norms to demand rights for sex workers, including suggestions for legalisation of prostitution, which are seen as allowing women in the trade rights to protection from the police, pimps and the right to get legal credit and health care.

> All men feel hungry for sex. Prostitutes prevent women from good families from getting raped. If prostitutes were not there, women would not be able to walk on the road. Unmarried young men would attack any woman on the road. In fact in my opinion, prostitutes are social workers, next only to mothers and should be treated with respect. [10]

---

8   The Prevention of Pushing and Forcing a Girl Child into the Flesh Trade and Immoral Traffic Act, 2005 is being tabled before Parliament in 2006; while the outcome is unknown it appears that it is likely to be passed.

9   Interview with Police Inspector V. G. Wagh, Nagpada Police Station on 5 November 1995.

10   Interview with Khairati Ram Bhola, Bhartiya Patita Udhar Samiti, New Delhi on 18 August 1998.

Some activists working with sex workers oppose the licensing of prostitution, suggesting that legalisation can only lead to further stigmatisation of sex workers, as it will create a division between legal and illegal prostitutes, will increase state control over the lives of sex workers. There is also a view that licensing of prostitution will legitimise the human rights violations that are part of the Indian sex trade, including the high degree of vulnerability of women within the profession, large-scale coercion and trafficking of minor girls into prostitution, the inhuman conditions of life within brothels.[11]

Policy makers in India however, seem more concerned about controlling women in prostitution, rather than engaging in some of these valid ongoing debates. The construction of women in the sex trade as immoral leads to a official perception that prostitutes are incapable of looking after their children adequately, therefore State efforts have focused on controlling the number of children a prostituted woman can have. A government schedule was passed in 1993 ruled that if a prostitute with more than two children has not got herself sterilised, her children would not be denied admission into schools.[12] Where sex workers do have children, laws aim to minimise their role as care givers. Under the Juvenile Justice Act, 1986, the State is empowered to evolve a system for the protection, development and rehabilitation of what are defined as 'neglected juveniles', which includes by definition, children of prostitutes. The latter, by virtue of their parentage, are deemed 'neglected juveniles'. A report by the Department of Women and Child Welfare similarly examines ways in which children can be removed from red light areas, using 'persuasion and motivation', rather than coercion (Department of Women and Child Development 1998, 5).

While policies and law are clearly against the interests of women in the sex trade, prostitutes believe that members of the judiciary also perceive prostitution as a 'law and order problem' rather than considering the 'human aspects of the problem' (Central Social Welfare Board 1996, 86–7).

A judgment on child prostitution brings out the prurient and voyeuristic attitude of judges, where children working within prostitution are described simultaneously as 'unfortunate' and 'girls in full bloom'. Speaking of the Immoral Trafficking in Women and Girls (Prevention) Act, 1986, it is suggested that the act aims to 'rescue the fallen women and girls...and also to provide an opportunity to these fallen victims so that they could become decent members of society', therefore prostitution is conceptualised as a violation of 'all canons of morality, decency and dignity of humankind' (Writ Petition (Criminal) Number 421 of 1989). The focus is on morality, rather than redressing physical and mental violence experienced by children within prostitution.

Official attitudes may thus hold that prostitutes fulfill an important social need, but women in prostitution are seen as embodying a dangerous sexuality, therefore they are still subjected to regulation, and control by the police and the judiciary. The

---

11   Communication with Priti Patkar, Prerana on 4 July 1998.

12   Interview with Khairati Ram Bhola, Bhartiya Patita Udhar Samiti, New Delhi on 18 August 1998.

concern is to allow prostitution, but to get women off the streets. PITA is therefore used almost exclusively against women practitioners, not against clients, though the latter are more threatening, and a self-evident public nuisance.[13]

Efforts to keep prostitutes under state control are evident in legislative efforts including bills introduced by the Maharashtra government in 1994. While making a token nod to feminist language, the bill stigmatises prostitutes by proposing that all prostitutes be registered under a Board, enabling composure medical testing and branding with indelible ink those who test HIV positive (Maharashta Protection of Commercial Sex Workers Act, 1994.).[14] Anti prostitution laws, therefore seek to regulate prostitution and the bodies of prostitutes. The purpose is not to improve the working conditions of prostitutes. Nor is there any concern for their health, except in the one area where it would, in the perception of the lawmakers, affect the health of the public that is sexual health.

Anti prostitution laws raise another area of concern. The definition of prostitution being nebulous, they invite an interrogation of every female body. Since the law does not define who a prostitute is, the police is given the right to arrest and prosecute any woman under this act who does not conform to social standards, as defined by the police (Patel 1994, 107–119). The term 'soliciting' is also vaguely defined, and the police admit that it is used to penalise any woman even within her home:

Sitting near a window, or standing in the balcony, gesticulating peculiarly, and combing her hair while near a window can be technically interpreted as soliciting. The police need a search warrant to enter a brothel. No such document is required to book a woman for soliciting.[15]

Women are judged according to their dress, behavior and other variables. Once defined as a prostitute, the woman's body is seen as accessible to all. Prostitutes all over the world have recognised this trend. As a collective of prostitutes in France wrote in 1980:

And make no mistake: prostitution laws are not only about prostitutes. They keep all women under control. At any time, any woman can be branded as a whore and treated like one. Each woman has to watch in her own life whether what she is doing is "good" or "bad", to censor her movements, behavior and appearance (Jaget 1980, 14).

Validating this belief is a ban on women dancing in bars and restaurants in Maharashtra imposed in 2005. While bar dancers do not always work as 'prostitutes' (in that they may or may not sell sex in addition to dancing in bars), popular social understanding of women working as bar dancers is that they are part of the sex trade. Mumbai based

---

13   Interview with Gopika Solanki, activist, Forum against Oppression of Women on 23 January 1994.

14   The bill has not been passed due to protests by women's organisations, but reflects the concerns of the state to control prostitutes for the sake of 'public health.'

15   Interview with Police Inspector V. G. Wagh, Nagpada Police Station on 5 November 1995.

feminists have argued that this displays the ambivalence with which bar dancers are seen, and banning bar dancing is therefore an effort to regulate sexuality of women, and is the result of 'middle class morality' that paints all women working as bar dancers as 'evil' or exploited (RCWS and FAOW 2005, 4). However in a recent court case challenging the legal ban on bar dancing in Mumbai, the legal defence by the bar dancers' union was that that bar dancers were not sex workers, and therefore had the right to livelihood. While some of the feminists involved in the movement believed that sex workers too have the right to livelihood, there was a feeling that making this argument in the court would weaken their case (Kale 2006). Therefore a strategic decision was made to remove the debate from the complexities of discourses on the shifting nature of sex work – which may have worked in their favour as the union won the case in the High Court – in order to protect the livelihoods of women working in the bars.

Pornography, obscenity or immorality?

Radical feminists have long argued that there are close links between pornography and prostitution, as pornography depicts what is routine within prostitution (Dworkin 1981, 203–217). In India, however, there is no legal provision against pornography, but the issue of sexual representation of women's bodies is legally addressed under laws penalizing obscenity. Therefore obscenity is defined as:

> ...a book, pamphlet, paper, writing, drawing, painting, representation, figure or any object shall be deemed to be deemed to be obscene if it is lascivious or appeals to the prurient interests or if its effect...is such as to tend to deprave and corrupt persons who are likely, having regard to all relevant circumstances to read, see or hear the matter contained or embodied in it (Section 292 IPC 1860).

The problems with this law are twofold. One, it does not explicitly define that which could 'tend to deprave', leaving it to the discretion of individual judges. Secondly, it does not specifically address violent or sexually explicit representation of women.

Bringing the representation of women within the ambit of the law was a contribution of the Indian feminists, who launched a campaign against certain representations of women. While the campaign shall be dealt with later in this chapter, but here it will suffice to mention that the response to the campaign was to introduce the Indecent Representation of Women (Prohibition) Act in 1986.

The law did not fulfill the demands or aspirations of the campaign. It introduces within debates on representation, the concept of 'indecency', a term with moralistic undertones. Feminists have argued that words such as 'indecency' and 'obscenity' are based on abstract concepts of morality and ethics, not on material conditions, and that the law places undue emphasis on 'immoral' or 'lascivious' representations, but does not focus on violent and degrading images of women that fall outside sexually explicit representations. In addition the obsessive focus on curbing nudity and sexual representations could curb women's expressions of sexuality. The issue seems of particular significance in the 1990s, representations of women that are sexually explicit, but potentially challenging to patriarchy have been legally and otherwise challenged by anti feminist and reactionary forces (Gandhi 1989, 377–85). The law also has potential for being exploited by communal forces, as it leaves out of its ambit any representation that is 'kept or used for religious purposes', including representations on temples, or any car used to convey idols, or for any religious purposes (The Indecent Representation of Women (Prohibition) Act 1986, Section 4). In addition, the 1986 Act increases the power of the state in the lives of private individuals, extending the power to any gazetted officer to enter the house or office of a citizen, provided that they believe that the citizen concerned possesses material prosecutable under this law. In effect, it would mean that even if the courts were to subsequently decide that the material is not 'indecent', its publication would suffer. A parallel has been drawn between this act and draconian acts such as the Prevention of Terrorism and Disruptive Activities Act (TADA) and the National Security Act (NSA), both of which have been used to harass, terrorise and silence innocent people (Kishwar and Vanita 1988, 38–39).[16]

Following the 1986 Act, the government also passed guidelines, aimed at preventing certain kinds of depictions of women in advertisements on TV, which did not extend to films, programmes and serials shown on TV. The code stated:

> No advertisement will be permitted which in its depiction of women violates the constitutional guarantees to all citizens, such as equality of status and opportunity, and dignity of the individual. In particular, no advertisement shall be permitted which projects a derogatory image of women. Women should not be portrayed in a manner that emphasises passive, submissive qualities, and encourages them to play a subordinate role in the family. The portrayal of men and women should not encourage mutual disrespect between the sexes. Advertisers shall ensure that the portrayal of the female form is tasteful and aesthetic, and is well within the established norms of good taste and decency (Doordarshan 1987).

The guidelines seem to influenced in part by feminist understandings of women's representations, as they are based on ideas of equal rights of women within the family and outside it. However, there seems to be an implicit belief that 'good taste' and 'decency' are part of a value system commonly shared. In actuality, the implementation of the code has been left to bureaucrats, who implement the code in very rare cases.

Neither the Code, not the 1986 Act have been implemented effectively, or taken seriously even by the state. For, the 1986 Act was not published in the official gazette

---

16　According to the Human Rights' Watch, 'TADA led to tens of thousands of politically motivated detentions, torture, and other human rights violations...Over 76,000 people were arrested while TADA was in force from 1987 to 1995. The conviction rate for these arrests was less than one percent.' (Human Rights Watch 2001). Due to popular opposition to the act by human rights organisation, the Indian government let TADA lapse in 1995. However, due to 'national security concerns' and fears of international terrorism the Indian government introduced the Prevention of Terrorism Ordinance (POTO) in 2001, which has also been opposed by civil rights groups.

or formalised into law for two years after it was first passed (Ankleswar Aiyer 1987). This indicates what one sees as a trademark pattern of the Indian state, a knee jerk reaction to a perceived threat. In this case, the threat was possibly the criticism that the government had faced following the passing of the Muslim women (Protection of Rights Upon Divorce) Bill, 1986. It can be argued that the Congress (I) government used the campaign of women's groups against 'obscene' films and posters as an entry point to pass the bill against representation in order to conciliate feminist opinion and to distract women's movements from various anti feminist measures implemented by the state.

The 1986 Act has not been extensively tested in the courts in my period of study. However, in 1989, the Bombay High court heard a case involving a Hindi film, 'Pati Parmeshwar' (literally *My Husband is a God*). The film depicted the heroine of the film as constantly servile to her husband, accepting and glorifying the violence meted out to her by her husband and his family. The film was denied a certificate for viewing under the Cinematography Act, 1962, on the ground that it violated a section of the Act that states that 'visuals, words depicting women in ignoble servility to men, or glorifying such servility as a praise worthy quality of women are not represented' (The Cinematography Act 1962, Guideline 2 (IV–a)). The producer of the film held that the refusal of the Censor Board to grant a viewing certificate violated his Fundamental Right to freedom of speech and expression guaranteed under Article 19 (1) (a) of the constitution.

Four judges in the Bombay High Court heard the case. Three judges held that the projection of the leading actress did not violate the guidelines. Justice Pratap stated that far from being servile, the heroine exhibited a praiseworthy commitment in saving her marriage, and the domestic violence suffered by her was 'ennobling;. Justice Aggarwal held that the guideline 2 (IV–a) was unconstitutional as it violated Article 19(a). He stated further that even if the guideline was constitutional, the characterization of the heroine did not violate it, as servility is not 'ignoble, but worthy of praise'. Justice Shah did not find the characterization 'ignoble' or 'indecent' since he reasoned that the film would be seen by a primarily Hindu audience. Only one judge disagreed with this reading of the film, reasoning that heroine was depicted as servile therefore the film violated the relevant guideline (Jaisingh 1989, 6). The judgment therefore explicates how ideal wifely behaviour is conceptualised in judicial discourse, which is based on normative notions that wifely servility and acceptance of domestic violence is 'ennobling' and 'worthy of praise', especially when displayed by Hindu women is disturbing. It also marks the film as viewable by a Hindu audience, whose shared cultural attitudes to women would see this projection as positive, and empowering, thus homogenising all people born as Hindus and marginalising 'non Hindu' opinions or perceptions. Therefore the communalisation of the case – as an issue relevant only or primarily to Hindus – is a way of silencing any opposition to the film, or to the judgment, and feminist opposition to the values displayed in the film as worthwhile can be rejected as 'western', and lacking a perception of Hindu traditions.

While Hindu married women are projected as devout and faithful wives, willingly accepting oppression at the hands of their husbands and other family members, judgements in cases of obscenity project a different, specifically 'Indian' sensibility of beauty, which is not seen as obscene or pornographic. In a 1980 case involving a case filed against a film, Satyam Shivam Sunderam for its sexualised content, the judge stated:

> The world's greatest paintings, sculptures, songs and dances, India's lustrous heritage, lofty epics, luscious in patches, may be asphyxiated by law, if prudes and pigs and state moralists prosecute paradigms, and prescribe heterodoxies (Raj Kapoor v. State 1980, 258).

These judgments display a particular attitude to sexuality, that of discomfort with some sexual images, those seen as western. Some 'Indian' or 'Hindu' representations of women, whether sexually explicit or not, are not understood to be 'obscene' or immoral or degrading to women. However, as we will examine in the next section, the feminist perceptions of pornography and obscenity are not devoid of some kinds of prudery that have the ultimate effect of reducing the spaces available to women. I contend that a focus on sexual imagery alone as 'obscene', both by the state, and by the women's movement has led to a situation where non-sexual images, however violent and degrading are not addressed.

The feminist movements and sexuality

> Why, in the first place, is it so difficult to talk about sexuality and why is it so necessary to do it all the same?...In India, the need to discuss sexuality seems to emerge much more as a tail piece to the discussion of fertility and fertility control (Dietrich 1992, 22).

It has often been suggested that within Indian feminisms, that the focus on legal rights and on violence against women in the 1980s and 1990s created a narrow and somewhat rigid view of sexuality, which focused on 'negative' aspects of women's sexuality, in the context of discussions on rape, adultery and reproductive rights of women, rather than as an important part of Indian women's lives. Where issues relating to the sexual choices of women are raised, feminist response had often been defensive – stating that sexual choices such as lesbianism are 'Indian' – or verging on rejection of such choices – therefore discomfort with claims of sex work as 'positive sexuality'.

Compulsory heterosexuality as a feminist issue

Lesbian activists in India in the early 1990s condemned the IWM as being 'homophobic' (Thadani, cited in Menon 1995a, 100), a label taken seriously by some feminists. One can sense the nascent, hesitant questioning of 'unconsciously' held ideas in the following statement by FAOW:

> It is true that sexuality has a very important place in our lives and so far, we have been taught to only think of heterosexual, preferably monogamous relationships...Lesbian

relationships are perceived by some as an alternative to the destructive violence and power play in heterosexual relationships (FAOW 1989, 14).

This somewhat romanticised view of lesbianism as being an alternative, somehow intrinsically more egalitarian lifestyle is reflected in the legal campaigns initiated by this group. The move to legally regulate same sex relationships has been proposed in a draft of gender just laws first put forward in 1989, later revised in 1995. The draft, in a somewhat awkward turn of phrase calls same sex relationships 'homo-relational realities', and opines that:

> Since contracts (between people of the same sex) are to be considered on par with each other, the partners in such contracts have similar rights...we are considering it to be a contract between two people of the same sex, and so there is no clear cut power relation as in the case of a man and a woman (FAOW 1995, 15).

The implicit assumption, that there need not be power imbalances between same sex partners glosses over the realities of many relationships, and ignores the ways in which power is experienced on the basis of differences in class, caste, age and religion. The radical potential of lesbian relationships is overstated in some of these debates, which have sometimes been projected as politically, and morally superior to male homosexual relationships (see India Centre for Human Rights and Law 1992).

Gay rights activists have pointed out that male homosexuality too threatens patriarchy, though in ways different from lesbianism (Aids Bhed Bhav Virodhi Andolan, 1991, 22). Section 377 IPC in its articulation reveals a deep-seated discomfort with male homosexuality, while choosing to ignore lesbianism completely, and it has been argued that the 'legal erasure' of lesbian sexuality gives women a social space to relate to each other sexually which is denied to male homosexuals.[17]

Between the 1970s and the 1990s therefore, there have been 2 strands within Indian feminism; one that had ignored the issue of lesbianism, and the other that has raised it in strategic, and initially in informal ways (Bacchetta 2002, 958). The issue of lesbianism was brought to the public domain in 1998, when a film made by a diasporic Indian, 'Fire' about a sexual relationship between two sisters-in-law in a middle class joint family in Delhi, was the subject of extra legal action by the Hindu fundamentalist right wing Shiv Sena and the Bajrang Dal. The film was cleared by the censor board, but screenings of the film were disrupted by mobs in many major cities in India, who projected the film as 'offensive to Indian culture'(Kapur 2000, 52–64). In opposition to this viewpoint, lesbians (and non lesbians) within the movement are quick to defend Indian lesbianism as being a part of Indian culture (Kapur 2000, 52–64; Bacchetta 2002, 958).

The issue of penile penetration has been the source of debate within Indian feminists and gay rights groups within debates on the Sexual Assault Bill (SAB) first proposed by some Indian feminists in 1992, and supported by the National

---

17 Personal Communication with member of Stree Sangam, Bombay on December 14, 1995. Name with held on request.

Commission for Women (NCW) also brings out some of the struggles over meanings within Indian feminism on issues of sexuality. At the time of writing, the SAB is due to be tabled before Parliament 2006, and proposes to extend the definition of rape beyond that of penile penetration into the vagina, therefore including a range of non consensual sexual activities, such as introduction by a man of his penis into the vagina, external genitalia, anus or mouth of another person; the introduction by one person of an object or a part of the body of another person; uttering of any word, making of any sound or gesture, or exhibiting any object or part of the body for sexual purpose. The Bill therefore introduces for the first time a gender neutral definition of sexual assault, introduces the concept of non penile penetrative sex as sexual assault and also includes the scope for a comprehensive law on different forms of sexual assault include sexual harassment. The SAB also suggests that as sexual assault under this law would be punishable whether it was perpetrated by a man or a woman, on any person, that Section 377 be repealed.

While members of different national women's groups such as Saakshi and AIDWA have been involved in the drafting of the bill, some LBT (Lesbian, Bisexual and Transgendered) activist groups fear that the gender neutrality of the law could lead to women being accused of sexual assault by men, which would add to existing sexualised control over their movements, and actions (PRISM 2006). In addition Mumbai based LABIA (Lesbians and Bisexuals in Action) has suggested that the gender neutrality introduced within the Sexual Assault Bill may work against the interests of gay groups; and demand instead that there should be a move towards laws that not based primarily on sexual assault, but instead on gendered assault. Representatives of LABIA suggest that while the suggested decriminalisation of voluntary male homosexuality is a positive development; the SAB introduces for the first time legal recognition of the sexuality of lesbian women; however this is in the context of violence that they are perpetrating. In addition they suggest that power within relationships is based primarily on gender differences, Therefore sexual assault cannot primarily be between members of the same gender. LABIA therefore suggests that sexual assault be dropped as a legal category, and replaced with the category of gender assault, which would include domestic and sexual violence between men and women, that is primarily based on gender differences (Shah 2006).

While the proposition above is strikingly original and interesting, there are some limitations. As in earlier debates within same sex relationships power dynamics within gender are ignored, or ironed out, which can be strategically important for a movement; however limiting and silencing for those suffering from these power dynamics.

Pornography and Indian feminism

The campaigns of the IWM around the issue of pornography reveal a parallel, unresolved understanding of sexuality. As activists have pointed out, women's groups in the 1980s had mainly agitated against films and advertisements that show women in the nude, or in sexually suggestive poses, therefore reinforcing 'the notion that anything sexual is obscene, and that respect for women is equivalent to treating them as asexual' (Agnes 1995, 137–8). The campaign involved the defacing of 'obscene' posters, a strategy started by the Chatra Yuva Sangharha Vahini, Patna in 1979. A Bombay based activist writes:

These tarring operations took place in most large and small cities. In Madras, the Pennuramai Iyyakam took out in 1982, a procession of around 500 women from workers' colonies, students, housewives, office workers who painted, threw cow dung, water and rotten eggs on the hoarding, and burnt magazines with offending advertisements. Without any deliberated networking, women just emulated one another in Bombay, Surat, Delhi and Ranchi. (Gandhi 1989, 378).

These efforts were met with ridicule and hostility from the general public, and what was worse, were coopted by rightist forces. In Patna, activists complained of men laughing and passing abusive comments as women climbed on ladders to tarnish posters. In Bombay, women from FAOW retreated in horror when they found that they had been pre-empted by members of the Bajrang Dal, who had blackened out film posters (Gandhi 1989, 379).

A few efforts were made by feminists to focus on non-sexualised, but stereotyped images of women in the media. These included focusing on advertisements that showed women in the home setting, usually the kitchen as consumers of domestic appliances; and men as heads of the families (Gandhi 1989, 379). FAOW also wrote a strongly worded letter to Doordarshan protesting against the portrayal of a divorced woman and of women's groups in a TV serial called 'Swayamsiddha' (The independent woman). The letter stated that the serial showed the protagonist, Nirmala as unable to cope with singlehood, that is, as 'weak, confused, vacillating, and dreading to kill a cockroach' while a feminist group that Nirmala meets was projected as insensitive and as a 'collection of well to do women indulging in social work, out of whim, not commitment' (FAOW 1998).

The central focus of the campaign however, has remained on sexually explicit depictions of women, and on legal remedies to counter them. In 1987, in Bombay, a booklet was published in Marathi, titled, Balatkar Kashi Kartat (How To Rape) by a journalist Anil Thatte. It was designed as a manual for would be rapists, presenting graphic details of the crime, some 'case histories', and the information that most rapists escape prosecution (Shah 1988). A women's group, Women and Media filed a case against the publishers and the booklet. Since the case could be filed only by an individual, not a group, Geeta Sheshu, a member filed the complaint. The case was not resolved in a judgment. A number of impediments blocked the proceedings. The lawyer for the publisher asked Geeta Sheshu a number of questions about her personal life, her views on pre marital sex, rape, etc. The public prosecutor did not object.[18] As in rape cases, the trial itself turned into a pornographic spectacle. The case was finally dropped, as the group itself collapsed.

---

18   Interview with Sandhya Gokhale on 2 March 2000.

An issue that anti-pornography groups have had to contend with is that of the viability of asking for a ban, or censorship. Censorship has historically been used to control women and free expression by rightist forces. Then there is the issue of how pornography can be defined in anti pornography laws. In countries where radical feminist anti pornography laws have been passed, the laws have been used against homosexual and lesbian material, as well as feminist literature that graphically describe sexual acts (i.e. those powerless in society). When the Canadian Supreme Court decided in 1992 to protect women by restricting the importation of pornography, one of the first targets was a lesbian/gay bookstore named Glad Day Bookstore, which had been on a police 'hit list.' Canadian officials also targeted university and radical bookstores. Among the books seized by Canadian customs were two books by radical feminist Andrea Dworkin (Strossen 1995).

While there have been some internal challenges to feminist understandings of sexuality in the 1990s (Ghosh 1996, 150–183, Kapur 1996, WS15–30) some feminists appear in practice to share the legal assumption that sex, rather than sexism is the problem, leading at times to collusions in views on sexuality between feminists and rightwing groups. This is apparent in the similarity between the rhetoric of the feminist Delhi based Media Advocacy Group and the Jagriti Mahila Samiti, a Delhi based rightwing group. The underlying assumption of both organisations on the issue of sexually explicit scenes and songs shown on satellite TV in the 1990s – an impact of globalisation – worked against social cohesion as it impacted audience behavior and was alien to Indian culture (Kapur, 1996, WS23). There were differences between the two – while the Media Advocacy Group was concerned about potential impacts of sexual representations on violence against women and therefore the concern was to protect women from sexual violence; however, the Jagriti Mahila Samiti focused on the perceived danger to 'Indian culture through these sexualised representations. Neither focused on violent and non-sexualised images that might be degrading from a feminist prism. In both cases, the danger is seen as coming from satellite TV, constructed as an alien influence on India. As we have seen, there is an ambiguity in the definitions of what constitutes Indian culture, and the unstated assumption that Indian culture is morally superior to western culture is potentially antithetical to feminist principles. As we have seen in the Pati Parmeshwar case, the construction of 'Indian culture' can, and often does include a prescriptive morality upholding the subjugation of women.

Issues of sexuality and feminist responses to rape

The feminist campaigns around rape also throw up similar unresolved debates around sexuality. As we will see in the next chapter, feminists have used the anti rape campaign to construct a critique of patriarchal constructions of male sexuality. Through the 1980s and the 1990s, there have been concerted efforts to expand the socially and legally accepted definition of rape as exclusively penetrative coercive sex, but to redefine it based on the experiences of women. However, feminist campaigns have also been forced to address the issue from within the parameters of state dictated discourses. This is clear when we look at a booklet brought out by a feminist organisation, which renames rape as sexual assault (Purewal and Kapur nd). The booklet tells women how to recognise sexual assault. The booklet states:

You have been sexually assaulted....if, against your will, you have been:

1. Kissed.
2. Fondled.
3. Handled.
4. Forced to have sexual intercourse.
5. Sexually violated through oral or anal intercourse.
6. Penetrated with a foreign object.

The law recognises only No. 4 as the very serious crime of rape, and all others as lesser crimes. But for women, all six constitute equally serious violations of their freedom and being (Purewal and Kapur nd, 3).

The aim of the booklet is to empower women by giving them a sense of their right to refuse men from having unlimited sexual access to them, therefore to redefine female sexuality. It also points out that women have the right to feel angry, and to take legal action 'because they constitute a crime. The state defines them as crimes, and they are not simply social misdemeanors even if men or society would like us to believe so' (Purewal and Kapur nd, 5). While placing as its point of reference, the rights and the experiences of women, the booklet breaks new ground. But, the experiences of women are, not, it appears, the final authority. Women are told that they have the right to treat the listed violations as crimes, because the state defines them as such, therefore the status of the State as the final and most legitimate arbiter is reinforced.

By stating the problem in this way, I am trying to address some of the dilemmas that legal struggle can create for feminists. For, there is simultaneously, an effort to bring all the experiences of women within the ambit of the law, and to undermine the authority of the latter. Nor is this recognition absent in sections of the IWM (Gothoskar et. al. 1994, 3022). However, as we have seen, some feminist debates on sexuality not only draw upon the state for legitimacy, but also share with it some assumptions on female and male sexuality. The debate on pornography brings out the moralism that is inherent in some sections of the movement. The ambivalence on homosexuality echoes socially constructed norms of sexual behavior. The debate on rape draws on socially and legally accepted parameters of sexual violations. On the other hand, feminist campaigns have re-defined sexuality in various significant ways. But, for feminist activists and theorists, it has been important to focus on the 'unconscious' and unstated assumptions of feminist politics, and rhetoric.

Chapter 5

'Custodial Rape' and Feminist Interventions

In this chapter, I will examine the feminist anti-rape campaign in the 1980s and 1990s, and state responses to feminist challenges. As we have seen in the previous chapter, the rape law defines female and male normative sexual behaviour. Here I will analyse the ways that official and feminist responses to three incidents of rape perpetuated on women by serving members of the police, i.e. the responses to the Mathura rape case judgement in the Supreme Court (1978), the Rameezabee rape case (1979) and the Maya Tyagi rape case (1980) conceptualised class and caste divisions. The three cases, individually and collectively, led to a major campaign on the issue of custodial rape (Das, 1996; Kannabiran, 1996).

The second section will analyse legislative debates preceding the rape law amendment in 1983. Following feminist campaigns on the issue of 'custodial rape', a new category of rape was introduced in the Penal Code, that aimed to legislate against rape by members of the police within their official jurisdiction, by public servants, by superintendents or managers of jails, remand homes, hospitals, on women under their custody. In such cases, the onus of proof was shifted from the defendant to the accused, which was a reversal of the generally applicable legal principle of innocent until proven guilty. What were the implications of this for human rights debates, to what extent do feminist campaigns prioritizing women's rights ignore, or avoid the issue of human rights? I will look at the influence of feminist intervention on the legislative debates leading to the amendment and the ways in which patriarchal and class based assumptions of women's sexuality played themselves out within these debates.

Next, I will examine the changes in the law, and its manifestations in the amended form through the 1980s and the 1990s. To what extent has the amended law benefited women sexually assaulted by men in positions of authority? Have feminist critiques of male sexuality and power impacted judicial assumptions?

Finally, there will be a study of feminist interventions on the issue of feminist interventions on the question of custodial rape after the amendment. I argue that the legal category of 'custodial' rape, limited as it is, has not been explored in its entirety during the course of the campaigns and in legislative and legal discourses.

'The policeman as rapist': Feminist interventions and official responses

Before entering into the personal tragedies that befell Mathura, Rameezabee and Maya Tyagi, of which rape was only one aspect, it might help to look at the legal provisions on custodial rape prior to the 1983 amendment. The rape law was enacted in 1860 as a part of the Indian Penal Code, and was drafted by Thomas Babington Macaulay, which reads as below:

> A man is said to commit rape who, except on cases herein after excepted, has sexual intercourse with a woman under circumstances falling under any of the following five descriptions:
>
> First: Against her will.
> Second: Without her consent when she is insensible.
> Thirdly: With her consent when her consent has been obtained by putting her in fear of death or of hurt.
> Fourthly: With her consent, when the man knows her consent is given because she believes that he is a different man to whom he is, or believes herself to be married to.
> Fifthly: With or without her consent, when she is under ten years of age. (Cited in Baxi 1995, 91–92).

The only exception to non-legalisation of marital rape was when the victim was under 10 years old. This definition of rape set out in 1860 remained unchanged until 1983. During this period, the law was not geared to take in to cognisance specific implications of abuse of power by representatives of the state, and was criticised as being concerned primarily with regulating the sexuality of women, rather than protecting their bodily integrity (Das 1996, 2411–2423). This analysis is vindicated by the three cases that I have already mentioned. I will therefore set out some details of the cases.

Rameezabee belonged to a Muslim family of agricultural workers. She was married when she was 17 to a mason in Nandikkotur, Andhra Pradesh. During a trip with her husband, Ahmed Hussien to Hyderabad in April 1978, she and her husband were arrested by the police for 'loitering' when they were returning from a late night show. The police demanded a fine. The husband went home to bring the money. During his absence, Rameezabee was raped by three police men. When the husband returned, the police beat him to death. Rameezabee was charged with, and convicted for enticing minor girls into prostitution. It was further alleged that she was illegally married to Ahmed Hussien and had married several men before cohabiting with Hussien (Kannabiran 1996, 120).She was, however, released on probation for a year, during which period she was directed to 'prove her good behavior' (Farooqi 1984, 186–8).

Mathura was a tribal, aged between 14–16 years, working as an agricultural labourer in Chandrapur district, Maharashtra. She developed a relationship with Ashok, who was the cousin of Nushi, her employer. Ashok and Mathura decided to get married. On March 26th, 1972, her brother Gama complained to the Desai

Ganj Police Station, Chandrapur that Mathura had been kidnapped by Nushi and Ashok. Nushi, Ashok, Mathura and Gama were brought to the Police Station for questioning, and to record their statements. At 10:30 pm, when they were leaving the police station, the head constable, Tukaram, and constable Ganpat held Mathura back. She was raped by Ganpat, and Tukaram attempted to rape her, but as Justice Koshal put it, 'was unable to do so for the reason that he was in a highly intoxicated condition'. Mathura came out of the police station and announced to the crowd outside that she had been raped. The crowd surrounded the station, and exerted enough pressure to ensure that a case of rape was registered (Baxi 1995, 46–7). The Sessions Court, Chandrapur, acquitted the accused, holding that there was 'a world of difference' between sexual intercourse and rape, and that Mathura had voluntary sexual intercourse with Ganpat, and had 'cried rape' in order to prove herself virtuous before the crowd, which included her lover.

The Bombay High Court reversed the judgment, and sentenced Tukaram and Ganpat. The Court held that since the police were strangers to Mathura, it was unlikely that 'she would make any overtures or invite the accused to satisfy her sexual desires' However, the High Court judgement was reversed by Justice Koshal, Supreme Court, who stated that as there were no injuries shown in the medical report, the story of 'stiff resistance having been put up by the girl is all false' and the alleged intercourse was a 'peaceful affair'. Mathura's testimony that she had raised an alarm when she had been taken to the latrine where the rape had taken place was dismissed as 'a concoction on her part', and Justice Koshal held that Section 375 IPC, only the 'fear of death or hurt' could vitiate consent for sexual intercourse, and there was no such finding (see Dhagamwar 1992, 46–7; Baxi et. al. 1979).

On 18 July, 1980, 25-year-old Maya Tyagi, her husband Ishwar Chand and two friends were driving to her parents' house in Faridabad, Haryana. The driver stopped the car at Baghpat Chowk to repair a punctured tyre. A policeman in civilian dress tried to molest Maya and was beaten up by Ishwar Chand. The police man returned with a contingent of policemen. The driver tried to start the car, failing which, Ishwar Chand and his friends pushed the car to start it. The police opened fire, and shot Ishwar Chand dead. Maya Tyagi was dragged out from her car, beaten, stripped and paraded through the town. She was finally taken to the police station, where she was raped by the police, and charged with being a dacoit. The police version ran as follows. Ishwar Chand and his friends were notorious dacoits, who had started firing on the police. Maya had supplied them with ammunition. The police, who had witnessed the 'encounter' stripped and beat up Maya. The police rescued her, and gave her clothes (Kishwar and Vanita 1984, 197).

The three incidents described above have several points in common. In all three cases, the victims were innocent of having committed any crime. Hence, the action of the police in holding them in custody was in itself illegal. Rameezabee and Mathura were socially and economically underprivileged. Rameezabee was a Muslim working class woman and Mathura a tribal. In both cases, their testimony was suspected, Mathura was considered to be a 'shocking liar' because she was 'habituated to sex', therefore it was concluded that she had consented to sexual intercourse with the accused. Rameezabee was similarly accused of being sexually promiscuous, which could be linked to constructions of Muslim women.[1] Maya Tyagi, though a middle-class woman, was discredited by accusations of being a dacoit. The three cases, individually and collectively, created a major civil society response on the issue of custodial rape.

Following the Rameezabee incident, there was public protest in the city of Hyderabad. The police fired on the protesting crowd, leading to loss of lives. As a result, a commission of inquiry was set up headed by Justice Muktadar, a sitting judge of the Andhra Pradesh High Court, which found the accused policemen guilty of the offences of rape, murder and assault. Justice Mukhtadar recommended that the accused be prosecuted for these offences, stating that the inquiry revealed the 'pitiable conditions of suspect women particularly of the poor classes at the hands of the police in the police station' (cited in Sarkar, 1994, 74). The Maya Tyagi case was discussed in the Lok Sabha on four days, following which the Uttar Pradesh government initiated a judicial inquiry (Lok Sabha Debates 1980a, 744–50; Lok Sabha Debates 1980b, 251–60; Lok Sabha Debates 1980c, 454–524).

The Mathura case created a major nation wide campaign on the issue of custodial rape, following the open letter written in September 1979 by four legal academics – Upendra Baxi, Lotika Sarkar, Vasudha Dhagamwar and Raghunath Kelkar – to the Chief Justice of India. The open letter questioned the validity of a judgment passed by the apex court, and described the Mathura judgment as 'an extraordinary decision sacrificing human rights of women under the law and the constitution' (Baxi et. al. 1979). The authors enumerated their reservations on the judgment, stating that a young girl could not be expected to successfully raise alarm for help when trapped by two police men inside a police station, that absence of marks of injury on Mathura's bodies need not imply absence of resistance, that there is a clear difference in law and common sense between submission and consent, therefore:

> Could not their Lordships have extended their analysis of 'consent' in a manner truly protective of the dignity and rights of Mathura? One suspects that the Court gathered an impression from Mathura's liaison with her lover that she was a person of easy virtue. Is the taboo against pre marital sex so strong as to provide a licence to the Indian police to rape young girls? Or to make them submit to their desires in police stations? (Baxi et. al. 1979).

The letter placed debates on rape within the rhetoric of violation of human rights. It also made connections with the Rameezabee rape case, citing it as another case in which poverty, class location and lack of effective legal recourse had led to sexual violence, which was legitimised by the State. In other words, an understanding of power in Indian societies was the underpinning of the appeal.

The letter was circulated among civil liberty groups and women's organisations, initiating a campaign on the issue of state power against women. Meetings were held in various parts of the country, leading as we have seen in Chapter 2, to the

---

1   See Chapter 3 for more details.

formation of feminist collectives in different parts of the country. In Delhi, feminists held demonstrations outside the Supreme Court, demanding the reopening of the Mathura case. A review petition was filed by women's groups to this effect, but was dismissed by Justice N. W. Untwala on 3 April 1980 (Agnes 1993, 111–2; Baxi 1994, 69–75).

The Maya Tyagi case was discussed at some length in the Lok Sabha, where it became an arena for conflict between different political parties: the ruling party Congress taking the official line of defending the police, and the opposition supporting Maya Tyagi. The debate was initiated by Ram Vilas Paswan, a member of the opposition who complained that he was harassed by the police in Baghpat, when he visited the area after the rape. Vilas' protests and feminist campaigning on the Maya Tyagi rape case, which took the form of public protests by hundreds of women outside the Parliament, led to a judicial inquiry by the UP government (Lok Sabha Debates 1980, b and c).The Lok Sabha debates brought out the contradictions in the way that sexually assaulted women were constructed. On the one hand, MPs from the ruling Congress Party, maligned Maya Tyagi as a violent criminal, and a sexually promiscuous woman, therefore non trustworthy:

> After the firing (by the police) took place, when these people had died, this lady was seen by so many people. She was throwing cartridges from the car...this lady, as per information, divorced her husband and married Iswar Tyagi (Shri Rajesh Pilot, Lok Sabha Debates 1980c, 478).

She was also dismissed as not belonging to a respectable family, as her family members had not applied for bail immediately after the arrest (Lok Sabha Debates 1980c, 480). The implication was therefore that a criminal and non 'respectable' could be raped with impunity. Those defending the accused articulated other stereotypes about rape:

> All those two to three thousand people followed the lady and the police to the police station...when those two to three thousand people were also present outside, how is it that a lady could be raped in a *thana*, and at a time when it was just...noon? How could she be raped at that time? (Shri L Bhatia, Lok Sabha Debates 1980c, 480).

The assumption here is that rapes take place only at the dead of night and that the police would be as caring of public opinion to desist from raping and torturing a woman in the presence of a crowd outside the police station. Given that the police had publicly stripped and paraded Maya Tyagi shortly before taking her to the police station, the intervention can only be seen as deliberately naïve in its understanding of state power against women.

While MPs opposing Maya Tyagi's claims based their analysis on sexist and class based understanding of Indian society, the discourse of those defending Maya Tyagi reflected other stereotypes about rape. Susheela Gopalan, a member of a leftwing party, added a rhetorical flourish to the debates, stating:

By this incident, you have stripped naked and paraded not only Mrs Maya Tyagi, but the whole womanhood of India (Lok Sabha Debates 1980c, 489).

Maya Tyagi's rape is equated with a loss of national honour, and she is no longer merely a victim of police arrogance, brutality and violence, but the symbol of all the raped and dishonoured women of India. However, Ishwar Chand and his friend, who suffered perhaps an equally if not more tragic fate, loss of life, are not projected as symbolic of Indian men, helpless against the might of the state. Therefore, the opposition felt by men and women opposing rape often stemmed from patriarchal ideology, that is, the honour of women and the need to protect it.

Some of these stereotypes about rape were challenged by feminists. FAR's analysis linked rape with male power against women, and the analyses was understood not only through a radical feminist prism, i.e., the notion that all men are potential rapists, but was combined, somewhat self consciously, with a 'deliberate, non accidental, and socialist' understanding. Therefore, following western radical feminist analysis (Brownmiller 1993), rape was seen as bringing out, and enlarging opposition between the sexes nakedly, unlike other forms of gender based oppression, such as lower wages for women. Rape, and the fear of rape was understood an instrument for terrorising and paralysing women, contributing to a low sense of self worth (Gothoskar 1980). Flowing from this, FAR argued that the rape victim should not feel ashamed of herself, since she is a victim and the rapist the culprit, and pointed out that rape was used precisely to inculcate a sense of shame, and to enable the present exploitative system to maintain the subjugation of women and the sexual division of women. FAR also saw a continuum between rape and other forms of violence against women, including wife battering and wife murder (Datar 1998, 23).

However, the FAR analyses moved beyond mainstream western analysis of rape in primarily interpersonal terms of an expression of male power against women. This was done by making a distinction between different kinds of rape, i.e., rapes during war, during communal or caste riots, during class struggle, rapes in work places, rapes by the police and rapes by criminals from the underworld. It was suggested that it was necessary to distinguish between these rapes because there are different politics underlying each. Hence, the methods and skills needed to combat them would have to be different in each case (Gothoskar 1980, 3–5). Significantly, at this stage, Indian feminists had a broader understanding of rape than the campaign itself, which was essentially centred on rape perpetuated by the police, which represented the most visible power of the Indian State during the period of study. While FAR's analysis of rape is limited in that that the raped person is projected and described as a victim, not a survivor of rape and the concept of custodial rape is not carried to its logical conclusion, as it does not include rapes by members of the army on civilian populations, nor are institutions of the family or marriage understood as being custodial positions, where men in the family as fathers, brothers or husbands enjoy positions of power and authority over women. Had this been done, sexual abuse within the family, and marital rape could legitimately be included in their analysis of what may constitute custody. Nevertheless, the analysis is nuanced and complex, based as it is on perceptions of power relations in Indian society. In contrast, we have seen that legislative debates conceptualise rape within the parameters of 'shame' and 'honour', which could well be the result of abstracting rape from wider critiques of patriarchy. Many of these trends are apparent in the following section, where I examine the legislative debates before the rape law amendment in 1983.

Rape law amendment and legislative debates

On 12 August 1980, a bill was introduced in the Lok Sabha that suggested major amendments to the rape law. Firstly, an amendment was made to Section 228 IPC that prohibited press coverage of any incident of rape, or any publicity that revealed the name of the offender or the victim, and the insertion of Section 228A that mandated that rape cases be conducted 'in camera', therefore they would not be subjected to and open to public scrutiny and attendance. Secondly, Section 375 was introduced in the IPC that redefined consent in rape cases as sexual intercourse by a man with a woman 'without her free and voluntary consent'. Section 375 also stated that the marital rape exemption would not be applicable in cases of judicial separation, therefore creating to a partial expansion of the category of marital rape in Indian rape law. Finally, Section 376 IPC was introduced, which created a new category of rape, that is, rape by members of the police within their official jurisdiction, by public servants, by superintendents or managers of jails, remand homes and hospitals on women under their custody. Gang rape was included within this category of aggravated rape, and all these categories attracted longer custodial sentences than other forms of rape. Significantly, under Section 376, the onus of proof was shifted from the defendant to the accused. That is, 'if the woman stated that she did not consent, the court would presume that she did not consent'(Bill No. 162 of 1980). This was a reversal of the generally applicable legal principle of the accused being treated as innocent until proven guilty.

The bill was referred to a Joint Committee comprising of representatives from both houses of Parliament, and various ministries, which taking into account the popular movements that had contributed to the framing of this bill, entered into debates with women's groups, lawyers and members of the press. After 44 sittings, the report was tabled in the Lok Sabha on 2 November 1982 – two years after the bill was first introduced in Parliament (Joint Committee 1982). The Joint Committee report supported the concerns of some feminist groups, that Section 228 and 228 A would prevent women's organisations from protesting against rape judgements and rape cases, as this could potentially identify both victim and offender, and that it would lead to an indirect form of press censorship (FAOW 1980, 1–2). Therefore the report recommended that under certain circumstances, publicity may be 'necessary for proper investigation'; therefore that publicity be permitted if the victim desired it, or it was in the interests of the case (Joint Committee 1982, 6–7).

In further agreement with feminist concerns, the Committee suggested that provisions regarding rapes by policemen be strengthened, that Section 376 be extended to all the staff of a jail, not merely the supervisory staff; that rapes in hospitals be extended to include visitors, as well as patients, that rape of minors be included under this section and that the rape of a physically and mentally disabled woman be brought within Section 376 (Joint Committee 1982, 9–11). However, on the issue of marital rape, the Committee took a somewhat conservative stand, suggesting that in the case of judicial separation, 'there is a possibility of reconciliation until the decree of divorce is granted, therefore non consensual sex between a judicially separated couple not be treated as rape'(Joint Committee 1982, 8–9). Further, it was recommended that rape of a minor within marriage be considered a less serious offence than other forms of child rape. In a note of dissent accompanying the recommendations, a member of the Committee, MP L.K. Advani[2] opposed the provision criminalising the rape of a minor by her husband, on the ground that rape within marriage should not be recognised under any circumstances, stating that:

> ...reprehensible though child marriage is, it surely can not be put in the same category as rape...We therefore favour an unqualified exception saying that "sexual intercourse by a man with his own wife is not rape" (Joint Committee 1982, 24–5).

The Commission's concerns and Advani's intervention in this debate exposes some of the anxieties of conservative forces about feminist interventions. Allowing marital rape to be criminalised, even in the limited area of child marriage and judicial separation was construed as a threat to the institution of marriage itself, which was constructed as based on the undisputed sexual rights of men over women within marriage. Even though Advani makes a token acknowledgment to 'modernity' by calling child marriage reprehensible, this is however contradicted by his subsequent words. In other contexts, feminists have argued that the socially sanctioned sexualisation of a child in cases of child marriage was the most reprehensible aspect of child marriage. Therefore, far from being treated as an exception; sexual abuse of children within marriage should be punished more severely than other forms of sexual abuse (Mikhail 2000, 43–49).

The Joint Committee made several general recommendations for the bill. The committee suggested that the right to private defence extended to causing death be given to a woman on molestation, as on rape. In addition, to safeguard women's safety, women should not be arrested after sunset and before sunrise; that medical examination of the accused, and of the complainant be done immediately on complaint, that social welfare officials be associated in the procedures; that compensation be given to rape victims to compensate for social ostracism. Many of these suggestions are based in social norms and notions about rape. As we have seen in Maya Tyagi's case, women's safety cannot guaranteed by not arresting women

---

2   L. K. Advani is currently a senior member of the Hindu fundamentalist right wing party, Bhartiya Janata Party (BJP).

at night, and the suggestion merely reinforces the notion that rape takes place only at the dead of night. Ludicrous in itself, the idea can also contribute to disbelief in cases when the incidents of rape do take place at other times, as is evident in the Lok Sabha debates following the Maya Tyagi incident. Another limitation of the Joint Committee report is that it did not take into cognisance the recommendations of the Law Commission, and of women's organisations that the past sexual history of the woman not be adduced in the evidence, or during cross examination.

However, the Joint Committee Report seems to be influenced in part by feminist rhetoric, and concerns. Similarly, during the course of the Lok Sabha debates, we see some degree of acceptance of feminist principles, though in many cases, it remains a token acceptance. In fact, the bill itself is recognised as the result of civil society responses and women's movement protest:

> Sir, a hue and cry was raised by the people and by the Press and it was taken up by the Parliament as early as in April 1980. It was on that basis that demands were made that stringent provisions should be made to punish those who are guilty of rape, particularly the guilty person having authority given to them by the state, namely the police. ...So, the public and the representatives of the media have been feeling that necessary protection be given immediately to women (Shri Amal Datta Lok Sabha Debates 1983b, 417).

Several references were made during the course of the debates to the women's movement, and the bill was projected as a 'gain of the women's movement' (Lok Sabha Debates 1983b, 465). The positive role of the media, and of women's groups in publicising incidents of rape was reiterated, and it was pointed out that the move to introduce Section 228A, debarring publicity would defeat the purpose of the amendment, by preventing the press and social movements from playing a positive role (Lok Sabha Debates 1983c, 357).

While feminist influence was seen by some MPs as being positive, there was also a sense in the debates that some demands were either 'counterproductive' or excessive. Therefore, it was suggested that women's organisations wanted the provisions in S228 and S228A, ignoring feminist protests about it:

> If the ladies want this (Section 228A), they are welcome to it. But, I would suggest that it is not in the interests of the ladies themselves, and I feel it is terribly counter productive (Shri Ram Jethmalani Lok Sabha Debates 1983c, 412).

There was some concern that women's organisations had gone too far in some of their demands. One MP referred to an appeal made to the Delhi High Court to review a rape case in which the accused had been acquitted, followed by demonstrations outside the Court, which was seen as not 'consistent with the rule of law' (Shri Ram Jethmalani Lok Sabha Debates 1983b, 410). The fear that feminists go too far in some demands was something of a refrain during the debates, most evident in the debates around marital rape. More than one MP expressed horror at the proposal to criminalise rape of minors within marriage:

The concept of rape within marriage is new. It is against our culture. In our country, in some parts, girls develop earlier. Even if they are young, their bodies are ready for sex (Shri Daga, Lok Sabha Debates 1983c, 415, translated from Hindi).

In a similar vein, it was argued that if child marriages were not prevented by law enforcers, it was 'absurd' to stop men from exercising their 'conjugal rights' within these marriages, and to expect the husband to become a 'hermit' (Shri Ram Jethmalani, Lok Sabha Debates 1983c, 415, translated from Hindi). The debate was therefore based on the social sanctity given to sexual relations within marriage. However the flip side of this assumption was the view that all sexual relations outside marriage were immoral and needed to be treated as rape, which as considered 'universal morality' (Shri AT Patil, Lok Sabha Debates 1983c, 367). The 'moral' position taken in this perspective denies women any sexual agency. All sexual activity outside marriage is deemed wrong and all sexual activity within marriage is socially sanctioned. Men are considered the initiators of sex within marriage, and the wives have no choice but to comply. Significantly, this position was not addressed or challenged in subsequent debates.

The feminist proposal that the past sexual history of the woman not be raised during the trial was opposed as another unreasonable feminist demand and it was feared that if it was accepted, false cases of rape would be filed by women, especially against rich and powerful men to malign them, perhaps at the behest of the police (Lok Sabha Debates 1983b, 431). There were concerns that not all women were 'virtuous', therefore such women were likely to lie about rape:

...after all, we are not dealing all the time with virtuous women. We may also deal with some women who, unfortunately, do not conform to the normal standards of womanhood (Shri Ram Jethmalani Lok Sabha Debates 1983c, 413).

There appear to be two implications to this argument. One, that 'non virtuous' women are likely to fabricate stories of rape. Second, that 'non virtuous' women cannot be raped, as they will not ever refuse sex at any point, with any man. This was opposed by only one woman MP, who pointed out that all women, including judicially separated women and prostitutes, had the unconditional right to refuse sex from any man, hence, the past conduct of the raped woman should be treated as irrelevant in a rape trial (Lok Sabha Debates 1983b, 431). However the rape law, when passed empowered the defence lawyer to make insinuations about the raped woman's sexual history (Section 155 IEA), however the same section was not applicable to the accused.

Male discomfort with feminist interventions is apparent through the use of humour to negate and undermine feminist arguments. It was suggested, somewhat facetiously, that the Joint Commission's recommendation that compensation be paid to rape victims was accepted, it would be an incentive for women to make false claims about rape (Lok Sabha Debates 1983c, 371). In a similar, if more salacious vein, it was suggested that the age of consent be reduced from 16 years, as contemporary minors had sexual knowledge and experience, thereby negating the impact of sexual abuse on young children:

> Furthermore, is it not a fact that these days, with the sex education, the girls and boys know the sex? (sic)....I have quoted many girls from the American magazine who are past masters at the age of sixteen. They have a lot of experience of sex (Shri A.T. Patil, Lok Sabha Debates 1983b, 377).

Legislators expressed fear at the possible outcome of the bill. One MP expressed his terror in these words:

> Sir, I do not know how you are feeling, but my first feeling is that, whatever may be the outcome of the Bill, its appearance is scaring (sic). Most of the speeches are positively terrifying. I would very humbly like to submit before this august house that we males are not that bad as has been supposed (Shri A.K. Roy Lok Sabha Debates 1983b, 377).

The Lok Sabha debates contributed to stereotypes about different religious communities. As we have seen, rape is seen as a denigration of womanhood. The discourse of the denigration of women focused on a particular understandings of Indian history. In one, ancient India was romanticised as a 'golden period' where Hindu women was constructed as enjoying a very high status. The decline in the status of women is attributed to the entry of 'Muslim invaders in the middle ages' (Shri Brajmohan Mohanty, Lok Sabha Debates 1983b, 422), therefore feeding into communalised perceptions of Muslim men being rapacious and posing a sexual threat to Hindu women. In a different formulation, the entry of modern society and capitalism is seen as the cause for the decline of the status of women. An MP representing the tribal areas of Dhanbad, Bihar, believed that tribal societies were far safer for women than urban cities, which was attributed to the economic and social freedom enjoyed by tribal women. Capitalist development was seen as responsible for the decline in the status of women, and increased violence against women (Shri AK Roy, Lok Sabha Debates 1983b, 401–2).

Both these perspectives are made from very different ideological stands – the first from a quasi nationalist, pro-Hindutva understanding of history; the second from a self consciously Marxist Leninist critique of capitalist societies. Both, however have one thing in common, that is they romanticised the past as being more egalitarian as far as gender relations are concerned. As we have seen in Chapter 3, right wing critiques of 'Muslim' societies and gender relations form the basis of rationale for sexual abuse of minority women in communal riots, as potential 'revenge' for past wrongs against Hindu women, as in anti Muslim pogroms in Gujarat in 2002.

Some interventions questioned and critiqued the double standards of morality that left rapists free of social stigma, but penalised the raped woman, for instance references were made to increase in child marriages due to fears of rape, which was linked to the notion that there could be no reparation or restitution for rape (Lok Sabha Debates 1983b, 442 and 446–7). What was not questioned, however was whether marriages could protect children from sexual violence. Linked to the recognition of social stigma was the appeal for compensation for raped women. Economic compensation was projected as a way to rehabilitate the woman, as marriage might prove difficult. The double standards displayed by society were thus accepted as a rationale for economic redemption, as social acceptance would otherwise be impossible (Lok Sabha Debates 1983b, 422–8).

The issue of custodial rape was addressed at great length, and some MPs pointed to possible nexus between corrupt police personnel and other sections of the State, that assured them of state protection (Lok Sabha Debates 1983b, 422–3 and 456). Similarly, there was an understanding that the State protected the interests of powerful and rich women, while the rights of working class women were violated with impunity:

> When rich, capitalist or feudal women are raped, the state machinery is expended in punishing the guilty. Such efforts are not made in the case of ordinary people. Ordinary people today recognise the double standards of law...This is not in accordance with our constitutional rights (Shri Rahi, Lok Sabha Debates 1983c, 386–7, translated from Hindi).

Therefore the Lok Sabha debates acknowledged the need for human rights and constitutional rights of all women to be recognised, while there was an acknowledgement that in reality, class and caste divisions prevented equal access to rights, and protection under the law. While human rights were a theme within the debates, the inherent human rights implications of shifting the onus of proof to the accused in custodial rape cases were not raised. On the contrary, there were suggestions that the proviso of shifting onus of proof to the accused be extended to all cases of rape (Lok Sabha Debates, 1983b, 418–218 and 469–71). It can be argued that this amendment opened the door to other amendments in the Criminal Procedure Code, including laws against terrorism in 1985, 1987 and 2002; which similarly allowed the onus of proof to the accused (Narula 2003, 41–68). While the rape law amendment aimed to protect the vulnerable victim – the raped women – by this amendment; the anti terrorist legislation increased the vulnerability of the victim, in this case the accused, and increased the power of the state over citizens.

As a whole, legislative debates reveal some patterns. Firstly, that feminist interventions and rhetoric had permeated in different ways within policy and law making. However, the understanding of feminist politics was most often incomplete, reflected in the failure to draw linkages between rape and other forms of gender oppression. For instance, if a critique of son preference and discrimination against girl children is missing, the early marriage of daughters is not a cause for concern in itself. The issue of rape of minors within marriage is diluted, and it is condoned and accepted as an integral part of Indian culture.

Judicial interpretations of custodial rape

In this section, I look at judicial interpretations in some cases of custodial rape following the 1983 amendment. As a study of the cases will show, the focus of the judicial interpretations remained centred on questions of the 'character' of the complainant, rather than the crime committed by the perpetrator, therefore reducing to a token gesture, the legal proviso of 'shifting the onus of proof' on the accused in cases of custodial rape.

A study conducted by People's Union for Democratic Rights, a Delhi-based civil liberties group in 1995 that looked at ten cases of rapes by police personnel revealed that in most cases, the victim was a working class woman. In almost all cases, the accused has been acquitted; some have been reinstated in their old posts (People's Union for Democratic Rights 1994). In continuum with Rameezabee and Mathura cases, the class location of the raped women contributes to her marginalisation within the judicial process.

This is evident in other cases of 'custodial rape'. In an incident of gang rape by the police in Pararia, Bihar (1988), a large party of police picked up the men in the village and pushed them in to the jeep. Nineteen women were gang raped. This was in retaliation to the beating up of a police constable in plain clothes by some villagers for being rude to an elderly man in the village. While the government of Bihar awarded the women Rs. 1000 as ex-gratia payment, the investigation carried out by the local police was perfunctory and incomplete. There was no identification parade, nor a proper medical examination, due to which evidence of sexual intercourse could not be established. This enabled the police to escape the legal clause in which the burden of proof would shift once sexual intercourse was established. Further, the ex-gratia payment was used against the victim, as the judge remarked, 'It cannot be ruled out that these ladies might speak falsehood to get a sum of Rs. 1000 which was a huge sum for them' (cited in Baxi 1995, 128–9).

As we have seen in Chapter 3, the mode of taking revenge for imagined grievances is based on patriarchal understanding of honour and shame, where the woman's body is seen as the repository of community, class and family honour. As in communal riots in Gujarat and elsewhere, these perceptions lead to a hierarchy of gendered oppression. Therefore, in this case, the men of the community were humiliated by being tied up and arrested, the women by being raped. In the shared lexicon of the police and the community, the rape fulfills the purpose of humiliating the men of the community, and by extension the community itself. By acquitting the accused the Judge upheld middle-class belief that the poor are potential, if not actual liars, accepting and as the judgement noted the defence counsel's argument that 'the women could not be equated with such ladies who hailed from decent and respectable societies, as they were engaged in menial work, and were of questionable character' (Baxi 1995, 129).

The well publicised Suman Rani case (1989) revealed some other impacts of the 1983 amendment. The details of the case are as follows. Suman Rani, a minor had eloped with Ravi Shankar in March 1984. Her family had filed a case for abduction. The police arrested the absconding couple on 31 May 1984 at Bhiwani Bus Stop on the way to Jammu, where they were headed. Suman Rani and Ravi Shankar were put in separate rooms in the Patram Gate Police post, where Suman Rani was raped by two police officers, one of whom was Premchand, who then left Suman Rani and

Ravi Shankar at the Bhiwani railway station. Later, Ravi Shankar was picked up by the police, and charged for abduction and rape under Section 366 IPC. In the Sessions Court, Bhiwani Khera, Ravi Shankar and the two police officers were tried together, and convicted on the charge of rape, the policeman getting the minimum sentence of ten years under Section 223 (Prem Chand and Anr v. The State of Haryana 1989, 1246). The Sessions Court judge dismissed the plea that Suman Rani was a promiscuous woman, hence the charge of rape did not hold. He stated that:

> As for being used to sexual intercourse, she was raped twice by Ravi Shankar and then by two hefty jawans of the Haryana police for two-three nights at Jammu. No wonder, therefore, if her vagina was found torn (Cited in Mahila Sanyukta Morcha v. Premchand and Others 1996, 800–801).

The judge then went on to make a significant legal intervention, based on a feminist understanding of sexual morality:

> And all things said and done, even a girl of easy virtue is also entitled to all the protection of law and can not be compelled to sexual intercourse against her will and without her consent. Offences of rape and other allied offences are created for the protection of fallible, earthly mortals and not for goddesses (Cited in Mahila Sanyukta Morcha v. Premchand and Others 1996, 800–801).

The Sessions Court judgment is noteworthy on two counts. One, that it upheld the view that women transgressing sexual mores, in this case, non marital sex had the right to legal redress in rape cases. However, Suman Rani's lover was convicted of rape even though she had not charged him of rape, and eloped with him of her free will. While feminist organisations praised the judgement, they did not conceptualise Ravi Shankar's conviction as an infringement of Suman Rani's or Ravi Shankar's sexual freedom. The Sessions Court judgment was overturned by the Punjab and Haryana High Court at Chandigarh in1985. Ravi Shankar was acquitted, as it could not be proved that Suman Rani was under the age of consent, and it was held that she had sex with Ravi Shankar of her free will. The conviction and sentence of the two police officers was confirmed.

The accused appealed to the Supreme Court. The Supreme Court did not dispute that Suman Rani had been raped in custody. However, Justice S Ratnavel Pandian and Justice B C Ray were reluctant to award the minimum punishment under Section 223, on the grounds that Suman Rani was sexually experienced:

> Mr. Mukhoty, Senior Counsel appearing on behalf of the appellant took us through the recorded evidence of the prosecution witnesses...the Medical Officer...gave his opinion that the victim girl was used to have frequent sexual intercourse and parturition and there was no mark of sexual assault on any part of her body...and (Mr. Mukhoty) urged that the victim was a woman of questionable character and easy virtue with lewd and lascivious behavior (Premchand and Anr v The State of Haryana 1989, 1247).

Based on what the judges called 'the peculiar circumstances of the case and the conduct of the victim girl' (Premchand and Anr v The State of Haryana 1989, 1247), the sentence was reduced.

While judgments like those cited above bring out the more obviously conservative aspects of judicial functioning, one finds that even seemingly 'positive' judgments can be based on similarly anti women sentiments. The central point of many rape cases is the insistence on corroborative evidence under the IEA, which is understood essentially as injuries suffered by the woman, or inflicted by the woman on the man. Many cases are dismissed due to absence of marks on the woman's body (Baxi 1995, 23–50). However, some judgments stated that insistence on corroborative evidence is tantamount to a denial of justice, which on first glance, appears to be influenced by feminist politics. In a case of custodial rape, where the co-petitioner was a Nagpur based women's group, the judges held that to disbelieve a woman, especially a 'young girl' was to insult womanhood, based on the belief that in India, unlike in the west, women would not lie about rape because they were inherently more virtuous, or more subjected to sexual and social scrutiny. Since the accused was a policeman, the judges held that the 'crime was compounded, and there is no room for sympathy or pity'. The judgement read as follows:

Ours is a conservative society where it concerns sexual behavior. Ours is not a permissive society, as in some of the western or European countries. Our standards of decency and morality are not the same as in those countries...Courts must also realise that ordinarily a woman, more so a young girl, will not stake her reputation by levying a false charge concerning her chastity (State of Maharashtra v. Chandraprakash Kewalchand Jain with Stree Atyachar Virodhi Parishad v. Chandraprakash Kewalchand Jain 1990, 889).

In an earlier case heard by the Supreme Court, the judge held that insisting on corroborative evidence was to 'cling to a fossil formula', suggesting that absence of injuries on the woman's bodies did not made the conviction of the accused by the Uttar Pradesh High Court unsustainable, as argued by the defence lawyer:

No woman of honour will accuse another of rape, since she sacrifices thereby what is dearest to her...when a woman is ravished, what is inflicted is not merely physical injury, but the deepest sense of some deathless shame...(Rafiq v State of Uttar Pradesh 1980, 1344).

Within this understanding, a woman's testimony is believed only if she is a 'woman of honour'. To the judicial mind, an honourable woman is a respectable married woman or a virginal young girl. In another case of custodial rape, a married woman was raped by a policeman, after being threatened that her husband would be arrested if she did not consent. The Bombay High Court acquitted the accused on the grounds that the woman did not raise an alarm, and that there were no injuries on her body. The Apex Court reversed the judgment primarily on the grounds that it could not be proved that the woman was '...a prostitute or that she was paid any money by the accused' (State of Maharashtra v. Prakash and Anr 1992, 1984).

Some feminists have argued that such 'positive' judgements should be viewed with scepticism., and it has been suggested that:

> Feminists must recognise the contradictory nature of the Court's reasoning. While we welcome the reduction of the corroboration requirements in rape cases, we must vigilantly reveal and challenge the problematic assumptions about women's sexuality that continue to inform these decisions. Feminist understanding of female sexuality and of women's rights to control our bodies stand in stark opposition to the patriarchal pedestals of "chastity" and "virginity" – pedestals that are securing the conviction of rapists at the cost of re-enforcing the very assumptions that subordinate and oppress woman (Kapur 1993, 171).

Judgments on custodial rape, following the amendment in 1983, reveal a number of assumptions about male and female sexuality, especially the emphasis on the sexual morality of the victim. Even in 'positive' judgments, where the woman conforms to the normative standards of ideal womanhood, the focus is on the loss of honour and shame suffered by the woman. Rape is legally conceptualised not seen as a violation of bodily integrity, but as a loss of family or community honour, vested in the body of the woman. Therefore judicial pronouncements understand female sexuality in terms of middle-class and upper caste Hindu sexual norms, and are characterised by a distrust of working class and non Hindu sexual norms. While all the cases of custodial rape involved potential or actual cases of misuse of power by the police, this element was not the focus of judgments, even after 'custodial rape' was recognised as a legal category. The cases are treated as 'routine' rape cases, negating the amendments in 1983. The low rate of conviction in custodial rape cases (People's Union of Democratic Rights 1994, 22) seems to indicate the benevolence of the custodians of law and order, analogous to that displayed by the patriarch of a family towards his straying prodigal son.

'Custodial rape' and feminist interventions after 1983

Feminists have recognised that the 1983 amendment has not yielded concrete results at the level of women's lives, especially in terms of interaction with the police and the judiciary. The following statement by FAOW IN 1990 brings out some of these dilemmas:

> ...the (raped) woman has not got support from the state – the police or the judiciary even after the amendment. The process of registering a case continues to be traumatic. The woman would first have to convince the police of her good character and morality. Then, she would have to submit herself to painful and humiliating medical examination. Since the provision that a woman's past sexual history or character should not be used as evidence was not included in the amendment, the rape trials continue to be harrowing

experiences. So, it is not surprising that most women do not wish to press charges (FAOW 1990, 8).

However, feminists have had to acknowledge that notions of chastity linked with rape are not confined to the state, or wider society, but are shared by sections of the women's movement.[3] In two separate cases of rape, in which members of left-wing parties were implicated, leaders of the party questioned the character of the women who were raped. One case (1990) involved the rape of an activist from Kashtakari Sanghatana, an organisation working with tribals in Dahanu, a suburb of Bombay, allegedly by activists from a rival political organisation, Kisan Sabha, linked to the CPI(M). Feminists were anguished to find that women members and leaders of the CPIM, with whom they had participated in several joint campaigns on varied issues relating to violence against women, did not condemn the rape. On the contrary, they denied that the rape had taken place, questioning instead the sexual morality of the alleged victim, preferring to conceptualise the incident as an attack on left-wing and democratic values. Despite requests from the wider women's movement, women activists from the CPI(M) refused to conduct an independent inquiry into the incident, preferring to join in a show of strength with the members of their parties (FAOW 1990, 8–9).

In Birati, West Bengal, in the same year, three Bangladeshi refugee women were raped. The state government, ruled by the CPIM, approached the issue as a law and order problem. A senior leader from the women's wing of the party, maligned the women's character and stated that the 'incident' was a case of gang rivalry:

> A group of anti socials attacked and raped Sabitri Das, Reba Sen and Shanti Sen, the three women who stayed in the unauthorised hutments along the railway tracks...Although so many women of that area...were involved in foul professions and such honeymoons of these women with the anti socials were an open secret, that day's events appeared to be a sequel to the rivalry between these anti socials (Shyamali Gupta cited in Sarkar 1991, 218).

Such statements demonstrated that the inherent malaise within left-wing and democratic forces, that worked with feminist organisations closely, but held on to notions of morality and immorality as defining factors in debates on rape. Therefore, it demonstrated the discomfort that left-wing parties have felt on some aspects of women's emancipation, and on acknowledging the extent of patriarchal ideology internalised by members of their own party. The private-public debate was therefore reinstated – left-wing party 'feminists' treated these incidents as a 'private' issue, one to be dealt with within the party (conceptualised as an extension of the family); while 'autonomous' feminists believed that a public debate on these incidents was as important as in any other case of rape.

Feminists found themselves similarly anguished when Bhanwari Devi, an employee of the State sponsored WDP in Rajasthan was raped in her village, Bhateri

---

3   As we have seen in Chapter 2 and elsewhere, the Indian Women's Movement includes women representatives from left-wing political parties, including the CPI (M).

on 22 September 1992. As we have seen in the preceding chapter, the case was also used to legally challenge the paucity of legal provisions for women in cases of sexual harassment in the workplace, but here we will look at the role of the State as the 'custodian' and the power dynamics involved in the incident of rape and the police and legal intervention that followed.

Bhanwari Devi was a member of the lower 'Kumhar' caste that traditionally worked as potters, and as a part of her official duties as a member of the WDP she worked to prevent child marriage. Following her actions of reporting cases of child marriage to the police among the higher caste and locally influencial Gujjar community, she was raped by Gyarsa and Badri Gujjar, while her husband was restrained by Ram Karan Gujjar and Shravan Panda, and was forced to witness the rape. Gyarsa, Badri and Ram Karan were all members of the same family. The local powers enjoyed by the perpetrators, due to their caste status in the village, enabled them to influence the local police, who proceeded with the case on the assumption that Bhanwari Devi was lying, therefore failing to collect valuable forensic evidence after the rape. Women's groups in different parts of the country, however, supported her case (Srivastava and Ghosh 1996, 20–1). While the women's movement campaign against sexual harassment in the workplace succeeded in 1993, this made no impact on the judgment by the Sessions Court, Jaipur passed on 5 November 1995. The five men implicated in the case were acquitted. The judgment based its acquittal on two planks, including a romanticisation of Indian culture and lack of forensic evidence. The judge, Justice Jaspal Singh stated that it was impossible that in India, members of the same community would commit rape together. Conversely it was argued that the 5 accused were of different castes (4 were Gujjars, and 1 a Brahmin), therefore it was impossible that they would have worked together, as according to the judge, rural gangs are not multi caste. He stated that Indian rural society would not degenerate to the extent that they would lose 'all sense of caste and class, and pounce upon a woman like a wolf' and that it was impossible that any Indian man would stand and watch his wife being raped when 'only two men twice his age are holding him' (cited in Gangoli and Solanki 1996, 22).

Bhanwari Devi's rape was a classic example of power rape, as she was raped by members of higher castes, whose caste privileges were being challenged by the Indian state, represented by Bhanwari Devi. However, in the conflict between Bhanwari Devi and the accused, the state machinery supported the latter by disbelieving her and her husband, and by not collecting forensic evidence that could have strengthened her case. Therefore the State, by not protecting its employee, protected the interests of dominant castes. The judgment itself was protested against, and an appeal lodged in the Supreme Court. However, what marks a difference in the nature of feminist intervention in this case, and an earlier case of rape was that feminist organisations and Bhanwari Devi have been closely linked during the campaign. Bhanwari Devi identifies herself, and is identified as a part of the IWM, this identity lending her an almost iconic status within the movement.

In the 1990s and in the early twenty-first century, therefore there has been a shift in the feminist understanding of custodial rape and power rape. One indication of this is the Sexual Assault Bill discussed in the previous chapter in the context of LBT responses. The National Commission for Women, which supported the bill acknowledged some of the problems within existing rape laws:

> The present law (on rape) has become so outdated in terms of language and intent that it fails to acknowledge the true nature of sexual assault. In particular, the existing law does not address the increasingly visible offence of child sexual abuse...a substantial number of child sexual abuse cases are occurring within the family (NCW 1992).

Therefore feminists acknowledged the need to recognise within rape law, power rapes happening within the family (even thought this is not conceptualised as custodial rape). The charge of 'aggravated sexual assault' includes assault by a police officer, a member of the Armed Forces, a public servant or anyone in a position of trust, authority, guardianship or of economic and social domination on someone 'under such trust, authority or dominance. The age of consent was fixed at 18 years, an issue debated within the movement, and seen by some as dangerous in its control of young female sexuality, and as potentially 'highly puritanical and moralistic' (Kapur 1993). However, the age was fixed at 18 years, because that is the age when Indian citizens are entitled to vote.

The somewhat uneasy compromise made here reveals a dilemma faced by feminists dealing with alleged rapes of minor girls. As the Suman Rani case reveals, even consensual sex can be legally defined as statutory rape if the girl is under the age of consent. This leads to situations where cases of abduction and rape are filed against men who elope with girls. Not only does this intensify familial and societal control over the sexuality of young women, it leads to imprisonment for their partners.

The debates around the Sexual Assault Bill brought to the fore many of the complexities within feminist debates on rape. Following the rapes of Muslim women in the Gujarat riots in 2002 by both civilians and police and army personnel, feminists have similarly pointed to issues of how political, communal and male power can work together against the interests of women (International Initiative for Justice in Gujarat 2003).

As this overview reveals, the IWM's understanding of rape has become increasingly complex in the period under study. While with Mathura, the 'issue' took precedence over the raped woman, with Bhanwari, both are important. The shift in focus from custodial rape to rapes within the family lends the understanding depth and focus. It also creates a continuum of empathy between the raped woman, and others struggling for equality, justice and freedom. In the process, the raped woman is no longer merely a victim, but is reconceptualised as a survivor and an agent for change. As Bhanwari Devi, in a public speech made in 1995 after the Sessions Court judgment put it:

My struggle is not for myself alone. It is a collective struggle for all the woman who have been wronged. I will continue to fight.[4]

There are however other trends that are less heartening. As we have seen, the 1983 amendment has not led to substantial improvement in the nature of judicial and police procedures, or marked a shift in sexual attitudes in rape cases. Besides, the rate of convictions in cases of custodial rape is low, giving credence to the view that stricter laws and increased punitive measures make judges cautious in awarding the full punishment available to them. In addition, as we have seen, feminist understanding of custodial rape as being limited to rape by policemen might have been governed by political exigencies in the early 1980s. However, an inability to extend custodial rape to include other categories, including rape of minors, or adult women within the family, and married women by their husbands, meant that a substantial area of women's experience was never centrally addressed.

---

4   Bhanwari Devi at a public speech at the National Conference held by the Indian Association of Women's Studies. Jaipur. 1995.

Chapter 6

The Campaign Against Domestic Violence

The issue of domestic violence has been one of the major campaigns for feminists in India. Both Indian and western feminists have problematised the specific nature of dowry related violence as being a specific form of 'Indian' domestic violence which has been seen as being accompanied by dowry demands (Kumari 1989; Rudd 2001). There are, however, diversities in the nature and the context of the struggles and campaigns around this issue in different parts of the country. In Northern India, dowry related violence and murders were the central focus of feminist activism. In Bombay, the focus was more on domestic violence, which included dowry related violence.

As we have seen, feminists analyses of violence against women is that it is one of the mechanisms used to control and subjugate women, and is a manifestation of unequal power relations between men and women, and is reflected in many fields of life, and is escalated by widespread sanction for violence against women, especially domestic violence. Through campaigns on domestic violence, feminists pose a challenge to mainstream constructions of the family as a unit where the members get love, support and status, and point to the violence that women often experience within the family.

The issue of domestic violence has been one of the major campaigns of the IWM nationally since the early 1980s. In the main feminists have defined domestic violence as including violence perpetuated against a married woman by members of her marital family with or without accompanying demands of dowry (Majlis Manch 1995, 1). Domestic violence remains the basis of activity conducted by several feminist centres in India.

The response of the Indian State in the 1980s was to strengthen laws that prohibited dowry and to pass a new law that criminalised domestic violence. There seems a degree of overlap between the State and feminist discourses on dowry and on domestic violence, which has been challenged within the movement. As we will see, feminist activism, legislative debates, judicial statements and police rhetoric reduce or negate the differences between these two often distinct forms of oppression.

There have been many excellent studies in India looking at the range of violence that women experience within the home and some of the factors that may impact it including class, caste and masculinity (Gandhi and Shah 1989, Kapur and Cossman 1996). In addition, studies have looked at the links between domestic violence and dowry, suggesting that dowry has been transformed in the recent past to a means of extortion by the groom and his family, often leading to violence and death (Kumari 1989; Rudd 2001). Recent work, however, argues that the links between dowry and domestic violence are neither obvious nor automatic but that domestic violence in India as in the west has other important social and economic causes and manifestations and that reducing Indian experiences of domestic violence to dowry can be essentialist and can lead to exoticising domestic violence in India. Therefore, seeking cultural explanations for violence against women in Third World countries when similar research conclusions are not made for violence against women in Western countries can be dangerous and counterproductive (Talwar Oldenburg 2002).

There have also been considerable numbers of research studies in India that look at the development of and effectiveness of domestic violence law in the 1970s and 1980s (Haskar and Singh 1986; Lawyers Collective 1992, Multiple Action Research Group 1992) and recent legal and feminist developments.

This chapter will address some of these issues – by debates on domestic violence law between the 1980s to the present (early twenty-first century), we will seek to examine whether campaigning for domestic violence law has indeed served the interests of feminist practice in India. The chapter is concerned methodologically with analysing legal and feminist discourses about domestic violence. I will initially look at the feminist campaigns around this issue in Bombay through the 1980s. Next, I will explore the legal and legislative discourse around wife battering and murder during this period. Finally, I will examine the shifting parameters of feminist responses and state responses to these issues in the 1990s and leading to the early twenty-first century.

Feminist interventions in the 1980s: Violence against married women in the family

I am Chandrika
I am Gayatri
I am Fatima, Banu, Uma,
I am Jayalakshmi, I am Saraswati.

I am one of those faceless women who die everyday in your morning newspapers and go on to become a crime number in the Police Station and then a file to be pushed around in the courts... (Poem published in Vimochana nd, 1).

As we have seen in Chapters 2 and 5, in the early 1980s, the efforts around the anti-rape campaigns in different parts of the country yielded some results in terms of generating publicity and the creation of a public debate around the issue. In Bombay and in Delhi, this campaign was accompanied by the exposure of domestic violence as a reality in the lives of several women. As activists in Bombay discovered, protests against marital violence and death exceeded those against rape (FAOW 1990, 17). Several reasons are cited for this:

Perhaps, the sheer number of women who were getting murdered or beaten within their own homes was far more than the women who were getting raped or at least those who were willing to press legal charges. The stigma attached to a rape victim was far more than the stigma attached to a battered woman (FAOW 1990, 17).

In addition, there was a greater sense of identification with victims of domestic violence than with rape victims. This had to do, perhaps, with the endemic nature of domestic violence, including the personal experiences of violence of some activists or their family members, therefore a sense of identification with the issue:

> Our own mothers, sisters, friends and in some cases, we ourselves were facing violence within marriage. So, we had no choice but to respond to this issue (FAOW 1990, 19).

Given that the cases of rape taken up during the 1980s were mostly those perpetuated on working class, and often illiterate women by those in positions of political and social power, and that most urban groups were composed of predominantly educated middle class women, the difficulty faced with the latter to empathise with the former is not surprising. One wonders if there could have been a difference if the activists had chosen to focus marital rape in addition to custodial rape in the campaigns. At any rate, it appears that experience plays a significant, if not central role in most feminist campaigns. Therefore, domestic violence was understood as a 'reality cutting across class\ community\ religion\ linguistic lines' (Abraham 1991, 61) In other words, domestic violence was understood as a shared destiny of women within marriage.

In the 1980s in common with western feminist movements on domestic violence (Schechter, 1982, Hague and Malos 1998), the focus of the campaign was to break the silence around domestic violations and violence. Some women came forward, sharing the pain of the violence suffered by them with other women, therefore trying through the process, to forge links between all women, those who had suffered and those who had escaped. One women wrote about this process:

> I was sharing my deep and painful experiences with a group of women I hardly knew. But I had a feeling that they would understand since they were committed to fighting against the oppression of women. The issues that we were involved with at that time – rape and wife murders – did not affect us directly. I felt that sharing our own personal experiences, problems and struggles would strengthen the group and the bond would become stronger... I thought, if I am ashamed to share my personal experience at a broader political level, then I would be a hypocrite (Flavia 1990, 33).

The process of breaking the silence was no doubt painful for the survivors of violence, but the newly created groups tried to create a space within which the women could articulate their anguish and regain strength. Support took on several forms. It meant giving battered women shelter, sometimes in the homes of the activists, helping them find employment. It sometimes took the form of extra-legal action – confronting the husband at his workplace or retrieving the woman's belongings. It often meant referring the woman to specialists (FAOW 1990, 20).

Feminists realised that most women experiencing domestic violence would approach feminist groups as a last resort, after many other avenues have been explored (Women's Centre 1994, 5). Hence, the cases that come to women's groups are representative of a much wider trend in society, and it was therefore important to combine support to individual victims with a wider campaign around the issue. A part of the wider campaign was to publicise the problems faced by women while fighting individual cases of violence. Victims of domestic violence had found that the police often refused to file cases of domestic violence on the pretext that there were no legal provisions under which this could be done, and this led to feminists all over the country making a demand for a separate enactment on domestic violence.

While in Bombay, a distinction seems to have been made between domestic violence and dowry demands, in some other parts of the country, there was some degree of blurring between the two. The demand made by the IWM at a national level was that a law be passed that prevented dowry related deaths and violence. Dowry has been understood to be a gift to daughters in upper caste Brahmin weddings, but are now an almost universal aspect of marriage negotiations in all communities and castes and is seen as a tool by families to enhance 'family social status and economic worth' (Prakasa 1982, 61), but has led to families of daughters suffering economic problems, increased pressure on unmarried women leading to cases where some young women have committed suicide 'in order to rid their fathers of financial burdens' (Prakasha 1982, 62). In addition dowry demands after marriage from husbands and their extended families have been seen to contribute to domestic violence, and in some cases to young married women being burnt alive by their husbands and parents in law, understood in popular terms as 'bride burning'. Such incidents are explained by the families as 'cooking accidents' (Hess 1999, 23), due to malfunctioning kerosene stoves, used extensively for cooking by middle class families in the 1970s and 1980s.

The centrality of 'bride burning' to images of domestic violence in India has been explained by the centrality of 'woman burning' in Hindu culture. It has been suggested that Sita's 'agni pariksha' in the Ramayana legitimises women's oppression in India.[1] Indeed an Indian feminist in 1987 drew a direct link between Sita's ordeal by fire, and contemporary 'bride burning' in a poem named Agni Pariksha:

They say, Sita the chaste
emerged from the fire
radiant and Beautiful
There was a Sita I knew
chaste enough, till yesterday
a foul charred corpse today...
This kerosene and matches test
is something that the Sitas of today
invariably fail. (Geetha, cited in Hess, 25)

---

1   The image of the 'agni pariksha' is the lynchpin of the Sita myth in the Ramayana, where Sita's chastity was tested by a trial by fire (Hess 1999, 23–24). See Chapter 3 for more details.

While the imagery of an innocent woman being burnt alive was a powerful motif for Indian feminists in the 1970s and 1980s, it has subsequently been suggested that the almost exclusive focus on 'bride burning' and dowry related murders was myopic:

All violence faced by women within homes was attributed to dowry by activists as well as the State. The initial demand was for a law to prevent dowry related violence. This turned out to be a narrow, short-sighted and wrongly formulated programme. Placing dowry victims at a special pedestal denied recognition and legitimacy to the need for protection against violence by all women under all circumstances (Agnes 1992, WS25).

This critique points to a broader conceptualisation of domestic violence than the one shared by Indian feminists in the 1980s. Agnes makes a distinction between violence suffered by married women at a general level and dowry related violence, and also alludes to violence experienced by single women within the home at the hands of other family members. The focus on 'bride burning' restricted the focus to violence suffered by young married women, with the implication that all other women were safe within the home.

Other than pressing for legal reforms, another means of feminist mobilisation was the introduction of legal manuals on domestic violence. Most of these manuals were written by social activists and were written in language that was perhaps deliberately simple. They included a lucid and critical descriptions of existing laws on domestic violence, and provided advice on what a battered woman could do in case of violence (Haksar and Singh 1992; Multiple Action Research Group 1992; Lawyers' Collective 1992). One such piece of advice is provided below:

What a battered woman can do:

If you fear that your husband might hurt you or your children, you should leave. You can stay with your parents, other relatives, or a friend. (It is not a good idea to stay with a married man as this may lead to allegations of adultery which could affect a court's ruling on child custody or maintenance.) Take as many of your possessions as you can, if anything is left behind, take along a few friends and get them back... Women's organisations too can help by providing women who will be happy to accompany you if you go back to your home (Lawyers' Collective 1992, 6–7).

As this excerpt shows, the purpose of such manuals is to provide practical solutions and advice to women in distress. Not all the advice given may be of direct relevance to women in violent situations, as the reality of Indian social life is that very few married women would be provided shelter or assistance by natal family or friends, nor is it safe or viable for battered woman to leave their home with their clothes and jewellery.[2]

The manuals set out the problems in receiving justice at the hands of the police and the judiciary. The implications of filing a criminal case against abusive husbands

---

2   Astha, a victim of domestic violence, interviewed on 24 October 1996. (Name changed on request).

are examined, based on the experiences of women. In most cases, women's groups are projected as alternative spaces, which empower women in the course of their struggles.

> A women's group is a useful place to turn to. They can help you to assert your rights by accompanying you to your home if you feel threatened. The important thing to remember is that *you need not be alone* (Emphasis in original) (Lawyers' Collective 1992, 29).

While several feminist groups do indeed fulfill these roles, some activists have confessed to feeling inadequate when faced with the nature and magnitude of dependency that victims of domestic violence build on the groups and on individual activists within them. In most cases, feminist groups can at best provide practical assistance during crisis situations and some amount of emotional support. As activists have found, women in vulnerable positions often expect answers to all their problems, and look upon feminist collectives as alternative families or husband substitutes. When these needs are not met, they feel betrayed (FAOW 1990, 20). Feminists have hesitated to adopt the role of an alternative family for two reasons. They feel ambivalent about providing the kind of support that an idealised family is expected to provide, due on the ideological critiques that feminists have evolved of the family and marriage, which legitimises the dominance of the husband over the wife. It may not be far-fetched to speculate that this understanding has led some feminist groups to reject a hierarchical structure, preferring the occasional chaos of collective functioning.

The implications of adhocism, however, can have severe implications for distressed women. In the absence of feminist shelter homes,[3] support centres are forced to send women to existing 'rescue' homes, run by the state or charities on anti-women lines. Where feminists have created shelter homes, as in the case of Shaktishalini in Delhi, the conditions imposed by the State, existing social mores and a concern for personal safety forces them to control women's mobility. The only other alternative for feminists has been to provide women with shelter in their own homes, which can be stressful for both parties, and have implications for their safety.

Feminist debates on domestic violence also had to confront the specific nature of domestic violence in India, where the role of the extended family including the mother-in-law in perpetuating violence is an area of concern (Seshu and Bhonsale nd, 3–6; Kishwar 1994, 11).

It has been suggested that in the context of Indian society, women attain power and prestige as mothers of sons; therefore a sense of rivalry with young daughters in law, who often move into the husband's parental home is inevitable. Madhu Kishwar has written extensively on how 'Indian' families are based on an idealised notion of the

---

3   A study of five state- and privately-run shelter homes in Mumbai in 1988 revealed that most such institutions had stringent rules and regulations that restricted the mobility of women. Women are counselled to be submissive and docile in their marital homes. See Agnes (1988).

mother-son syndrome, where a woman's status as a maternal figure is considered more important than that of her as a wife. The wife therefore is the sexualised image of the woman within the family, and is seen as less deserving of respect. Kishwar suggests that:

> Relationships with children are considered far more dependable, enduring, and fulfilling. This may be related to the fact that while as a wife, a woman is expected to serve and surrender, as a mother she is allowed the right to both nurture and dominate and is supposed to be venerated unconditionally. She can expect obedience, love, and seva (service) from her children, especially sons, even after they grow up. Unconditional giving brings in its own ample rewards. In her role as a mother she is culturally far more glorified (Kishwar 1997, 22).

Therefore, the role of mothers-in-law in oppressing daughters-in-law can be understood through a feminist perception – of feeding into patriarchy by celebrating male power; and by colluding with male interests in oppressing younger women within the family. As we will see, this understanding is not shared by the representatives of the state in the legislature and the judiciary.

Legislative debates: Trivialising the issue

A study of the Lok Sabha debates between 1982–86 reveals that, during these years, a great deal of attention was focused on the issue of domestic violence in the legislature. While some debates were focused on the need to pass efficient legislation, most was of a general nature. The latter was in most instances, a reaction to the specific instances of domestic violence and feminist intervention (Lok Sabha Debates 1981, 368–498; Lok Sabha Debates 1982, 305–306; Lok Sabha Debates 1983a, 415–74; Lok Sabha Debates 1983d, 367 –550; Lok Sabha Debates 1984: 328–371). Section 498A IPC that criminalised domestic violence was passed in 1983.[4] In addition, discussions around dowry related violence and murders led to the amendment to the Dowry Prohibition Act in 1986. These laws and amendments were

---

4   Sec. 498A ruled that 'Whoever, being the husband or the relative of the husband of a woman, subjects such a woman to cruelty shall be punished with imprisonment for a term which may exceed to three years and shall also be liable to fine'. Under this section, 'cruelty means (a) any willful conduct which is of such a nature as is likely to drive the woman to commit suicide or to cause grave injury or danger to life, limb or health (whether mental or physical) of the woman: or (b)harassment of the woman where such harassment is with a view to coercing her or any person related to her to meet any unlawful demand for any property or valuable security or is on account of failure by her or any person related to her to meet such demand. In addition, amendments to dowry related laws introduced provisions to be used in case of suicide by a married woman within 7 years of marriage, and under S 113A IEA, if a woman has been subjected to cruelty by the husband by the husband or the family within 7 years of marriage, the husband or relatives are presumed to have abetted the suicide.

passed in a spirit of providing justice to women and as a response to the protests by women's organisations all over the country.

Some legislative debates conceptualised domestic violence as a part of wider trends of violence against women, and the specificity of violence against women in the home by their family members was therefore sometimes lost, other than in the context of dowry related murders and rapes (Lok Sabha Debates 1982, 305–6). The need to include women's organisations as a reference point in debates on domestic violence was reiterated during debates preceding the passing of S498A, in the context of discussions regarding the provision that the report of an injury could be either by the woman injured, a relative by blood, or 'in the absence of such relative, by any public servant of such class and category, as may be notified by the State Government in this behalf'. This was criticised by communist MP, Susheela Gopalan who pointed out that the role of women's organisations, who had played a central role in highlighting this crime was being undermined in favour of public servants:

> Where is the provision in this bill to take help from the women's organisations? You say... there is a provision that public servants can give complaints. Who is the public servant? When the woman dies, why is it necessary that only the parents (of the woman) should complain? (Smt. Susheela Gopalan Lok Sabha Debates 1983d, 431).[5]

While some MPs demonstrated an acceptance of feminist views and intervention, in the main, legislative discussions veered around the celebration of 'Indian' culture and a reiteration of the misogynist position that 'women are women's worst enemies' as an explanation of mother in law violence against daughters in laws in the family, both positions trivialising violence against women. Therefore, in the first case, women were put on a pedestal, and treated with sentimental pity. In the course of debates on dowry related murders, the Deputy Speaker of the Lok Sabha had this to say about women:

> They (women) are regarded not only as equal citizens, (but) as the motherhood of India. You must respect the ladies of India (Lok Sabha Debates 1983a, 447).

Women experiencing domestic violence were therefore treated as pitiable and helpless victims, and it appears that for these MPs, women's rights were derived from their identity as real or potential mothers, that too, suffering mothers. This does pose an interesting counterpoint to other traditional views on motherhood, that of mothers as being strong and invincible against evil. Given the context where vocal and articulate feminists were resisting these stereotypes, and demanding rights as citizens, choosing to see women solely as maternal images seems an effort to avoid responding to the very difficult questions and challenges that feminists were posing. The discourse also kept out single women, who suffered violence within the home, as it projected violence as linked to marriage and dowry. Geeta Mukherjee, from the CPI, made an unsuccessful

---

5   A motion by Smt. Geeta Mukherjee to extend the scope of the bill was negativated.

effort to enlarge the scope of the debate to include single women and to reduce the emphasis on dowry:

> In our experience, it is not necessary that this phenomenon (of marital cruelty)… is…only connected with dowry, but with certain other things which are equally cruel leading to death. Secondly, I think that it is not only a question of husband and wife...Take, for example, the wife of a brother. If the brother dies, the widow still remains within the family...this woman is harassed, sometimes so much that very often, death takes place because of that harassment also. This should be included in 498A (Smt. Geeta Mukherjee 1983d, 470–1).

Significantly, on the issue of domestic violence, as with rape, leftwing party MPs share and articulate feminist positions. Mukherjee's intervention is unusual in that it takes up the question of widows and their position in society. Widowhood, so central in reformist and legal agenda in the nineteenth century (see Chakravarti 1989), has been less so in the late twentieth century. The issue of violence against single women within the family was however not debated further in the context of legislative debates. It is my contention that the invisibility of single women in legislative discourse is not accidental; it shows a discomfort with any image of women that is not tied up with marriage. Marriage remains central to the different religious traditions in India and therefore being married is extremely important to the self image of most Indian women. The debates therefore looked at the issue of domestic violence in terms of Hindu families, therefore the focus on dowry, which has been conceptualised as a predominantly upper caste Hindu custom that has been adopted by other castes and communities over time (Kumari 1989; Talwar Oldenburg 2002). Therefore interventions that critiqued Hindu cultural traditions were ignored, such as the following:

> This (dowry murders) is like an illness...It is because of greed. Muslims are not greedy, they give mehr to women…Hindu dharma revolves around money (Shri Sunder Singh Lok Sabha Debates 1983d, 483, translated from Hndi).

It was also suggested by this MP that there was a unity in the oppression suffered by Dalits and women.

This intervention – as in the case of Geeta Mukherjee – that critiqued, rather than romanticised Hindu families were met with resounding silence. At another level, discomfort with feminist rhetoric and activism is apparent in several statements that portray marital and dowry related violence as a conflict between two women – the strong mother-in-law and the helpless daughter-in-law. Some MPs objected to what was considered an effort by women parliamentarians to 'define in two parts' – i.e. women and men – the entire society, therefore to see the issue of domestic violence in terms of male violence against women:

> Can I put one straight question? Who is the mother-in-law? Is she also a male member? ...The mother-in-law not only insists, but also compels the husband of the poor girl to live separately...So, why do you look at the problem as male or female? (Shri NK Shejwalkar, Lok Sabha Debates 1983d, 441)

A careful search of the speeches preceding this outburst makes it difficult to comprehend the source of Shejwalkar's anger. None of the women legislators had articulated the question in terms that could be remotely be seen as anti-male. Nor was there any reference to 'dividing' the society into two categories. It may not be unreasonable to speculate that the M.P was responding to his own notions of what constituted a feminist critique of violence against women. In a similar vein, another M.P. holds scheming women responsible for crimes against women.

> ...where women are beaten and even killed, aren't women also responsible? Mothers-in-law and sisters-in-law are women. Don't women provoke and encourage men, so that men are forced to commit crimes? (Shri Ram Lal Rahi. Lok Sabha Debates 1983d, 511, translated from Hindi).

Men are thus absolved of the crimes committed by them and the responsibility is placed firmly on the women in the family. Women are projected either as innocent victims, as daughters-in-law or as controlling mothers or sisters who 'force' men to kill or batter their wives. In a swift reversal of logic, another M.P. holds that as wives, women have the power to influence their husbands by using their sexuality.

> ...Laws cannot change much... This (violence against women) can stop through social change, not law...You women influence men at night, you can persuade them to do things (Shri Moil Chad Dada Lok Sabha Debates 1984, 279, translated from Hindi).

Therefore social change is seen as possible by female use of sexuality within marriage, that serves both to trivialise women's powerlessness as young married women, and to introduce a salacious tinge to the debates.

Some suggestions were made to counter these debates, ranging from interventions that suggested the creation of an effective social security system that enables women to live independently, the need to set up shelter homes and provisions to ensure speedy disposal of domestic violence cases (Lok Sabha Debates 1983d, 444–484). While these suggestions were not taken up in any serious manner, they reveal an awareness that the problem of violence against women in the home is not episodic, but based on the vulnerability of women within marriage. As we have seen, the issue of violence against single women is raised only by one MP and not examined by any other member in the course of the debates, thereby invisiblising single women.

The above analysis of Parliamentary debates on domestic violence reveals certain trends. On the one hand is a partial acknowledgment of feminist influences. In the main, the debates bring out deep seated anxieties about the challenges thrown up by such interventions. It seems important to emphasise here that Section 498A remains one of the more sensitive laws dealing with the violations that women face routinely in the family. Yet, legislative debates, and as the following section will reveal, responses from the police and the judiciary reveal a high degree of hostility to feminist ideologies.

Responses to domestic violence from the police

Victims of abuse within marriage have found that the police is unsympathetic to women in cases of domestic violence. In 1992, the Joint Commissioner of Crime, Bombay, Mr. R.D.Tyagi issued a statement to the press that he had sent a written directive to the police not to register cases of mental cruelty under Sec. 498A (Abraham 1992), therefore negating legal remedies available to women in cases of domestic violence.

The apathy of the police can have frightening consequences for women. One litigant describes how the indifference of the police had near fatal results in her case:

> The children ran to call the police because they were really scared for me. The police came four hours later, after all the beating was over. I might have been dead. (Flavia 1988, 165).

There have been cases where the police have refused to enter cases of domestic violence until they are linked to dowry demands and property disputes. This, in the view of the police, increases the credibility of the case, leading to a number of domestic violence cases to be linked to fictitious dowry demands, which has resulted in weakening the case, and acquittals of the accused in court.[6] In addition activists have pointed out that the police explain their reluctance to enter cases under S498A based on the high rate of withdrawal of cases by women. There are several reasons that coerce women into doing so, which include refusal of neighbours and family members to give evidence against the offender, as the matter is seen as a personal issue between the couple and generalised pressure from the natal and marital family to 'save' the marriage.[7]

Therefore, some women use S498A as a bargaining tool. An activist cited two cases where the women had managed to register cases of violence with the assistance of the organisation, following incidents of domestic violence, and abandonment of the wife by the husband. Following the case being lodged by the police, the men initiated a reconciliation with their spouses, as they feared custodial sentences under S498A.[8] These cases point to an interesting and creative use of the domestic violence provision by women. In a situation of general powerlessness, women and women's groups have managed to carve out a space within which a degree of negotiation is possible. Some women use the law to threaten their spouses into 'good behavior', especially given that ending the marriage is not an easy option in the absence of State, social and family support.

---

6   Interview with Gopika Solanki, Social Worker, Special Cell to Help Women and Children on 14 February 1999.

7   Interview with Geeta Mahajan, Bharatiya Mahila Federation, Thane Branch. 19 June 1995.

8   Interview with Sindhu, activist, Bhartiya Mahila Federation, Thane Branch, 10 June 1995.

The police echo the social attitude that the marital family should be preserved. The general reluctance to enter cases of violence against women in the home is based at least partly on the desire to preserve the family. This can have different manifestations while dealing with women of different classes. While poorer clients are often turned away summarily, middle class women are advised to return home and not break up the home. The police also threaten clients that they will lose the custody of their children if they leave their house, forcing them into retreat. An activist with a feminist intervention centre points out that not only do the police fail to inform women about their rights, but they also resent the confidence of women who might know the law (Flavia 1990, 21).

Activists and litigants have found that even when cases are registered under S498A, there is a marked reluctance on the part of the police to conduct the investigation efficiently. In cases of murder, a significant part of the procedure is the recording of the Dying Declaration (DD). A study conducted in Sanghli District, Maharashtra reveals that in 49 cases of death, only 15 women gave dying declarations, which were recorded by the police or the district magistrate in the hospital. In 3 cases, oral declarations were given to independent witnesses. 'Unreliable' DDs – including those given to independent witnesses not approved by the State – are not accepted as conclusive by the judiciary, which ultimately favours the accused. Some of the reasons stated in the report for the judiciary not accepting the DDs are as follows: no reference being made to the DD in the FIR, the DD not following the standard prescribed format of Questions and Answers, oral evidence not corroborating with the DD, more than one DD being submitted to the police (Seshu and Vasant Bhonsale nd, 38–40). Therefore, the negligence of the police leads to denial of justice.

Communalisation and domestic violence

Access to justice from the police in cases of domestic violence is also influenced by the nature of and the degree of communalisation of the society. In the context of the city of Mumbai, Muslim women have found that their access to relief in cases of domestic violence following communal riots in 1992 has suffered. Therefore, while the incidence of domestic violence has no direct link with religious identity (Majlis Manch nd, 9), the manner in which minority women suffer violence, and the redress that they have access to differ.

An important part of this trend is the partisan role played by the police in the communal riots in 1992–1993 in Mumbai. Muslim women have witnessed and experienced police brutality during and after the riots. The complicity of the State in condoning violence against Muslims further isolates the community. As an activist puts it:

> The reality of being Muslim in Bombay cannot be wished away. While the police is generally not keen to take up cases of domestic violence, if the complainant is a Muslim woman, they rush to arrest the man. After the riots, women feel that their problems multiply after going to the police. The police, as a part of the procedure, question the neighbours, who are terrified

after having been subjected to torture during the riots. So many innocent Muslims have been caught under TADA. This is another reason why (Muslim) women keep quiet even after being beaten by their husbands.[9]

Some minority women approach generic women's organisations for support, counseling and legal aid in order to increase their options. In such cases, Muslim women have experienced alienation while narrating their experiences of violence. There are several reasons for this. Most progressive and feminist women's groups are controlled by, and run by upper caste Hindu women, creating a context wherein Hindu idioms, language and rhetoric are universalised as Indian within the feminist movement as elsewhere.

In such a situation, minority women have complained of feeling isolated within the movement.[10] This sense of isolation for minority victims of domestic violence is increased by the appearance of social workers and activists in the organisations, if donning the traditional Hindu symbols of marriage, including *bindis* and *mangalsutras.* This acts as a deterrent in creating trust and rapport between women of different communities, serving instead to intensify difference. Besides, in some cases, there is a communal bias apparent in some social workers. In a workshop on the rights of Muslim women in cases of domestic violence organised in Mumbai, a Hindu social worker, working with The Special Cell for Women, felt that Muslim women have a very low status, explaining it as follows:

This is because their religion gives more status to men. (Muslim) men can easily give 'talaq' and desert women. Muslim women are more oppressed and vulnerable (than Hindu women). Their oppression is sanctioned by their religion (cited in Gangoli 1997, 3).

As we have seen in Chapter 3 and 4, such images of Muslim men as being rapacious, bigamous and violent are based on communal perceptions of Muslim communities, and in cases of feminist intervention, leads to a belief that Muslim women are fated to suffer. This is apparent in this response of a Hindu social worker to a battered woman who had approached her through a feminist collective in which Muslim women play a significant role, where the worker is reported to suggest that domestic violence was inevitable in a context where men were allowed to be polygamous.[11] While the link between polygamy and domestic violence is neither obvious, nor automatic; and polygamy is known to be more prevelant among Hindus than Muslims (Agnes 1995, 3238–3242); the apathy towards women suffering from domestic violence is thus couched in communal terms, justifying inaction in the part of organisations.

The situation is exacerbated by the lack of real options in civil society for single women. While the situation for poor and single women in India is dismal, for Muslim women on the verge of singlehood, things are worse. For instance, finding

---

9   Interview with Hasina Khan, activist, Awaaz-e-Niswaan. 14 April 1997.

10   Flavia Agnes, Verbal Presentation, IAWS Conference, Jadavpur University, Calcutta. January 1991.

11   Interview with Hasina Khan.

accommodation is a very real problem in Mumbai, as in other metropolitan cities. To add to the high costs of real estate, after the riots in Mumbai in 1992–93, when Muslim families were targeted, several have relocated to 'Muslim' dominated areas, due to fears of violence, and because some Muslim families have found it difficult to rent or buy property in Hindu dominated housing societies and localities, leading to a virtual ghettoisation of Muslim communities. Community pressures in such a situation would make it even more difficult for single Muslim women to find accommodation. Given this, many battered women do not approach police stations to file a case against their spouses, as this step would potentially render them homeless. Activists working with Muslim women complain that they are denied access in government hospitals, that they are not given ration cards and that their children are often not able to get admissions in schools (Gangoli 1997, 11). In addition, the leaders of the minority community push women into complicity and traditional roles. Following the riots, community leaders in Muslim dominated areas made speeches where they held the women of the community responsible for the riots. They were accused of lowering the prestige of the community by filing criminal cases against their husbands, by not wearing the *hijab* (head scarf) and not praying.[12] Thus, as we have seen in the case of sexual violence during the Gujarat riots (Chapter 3), the generalised bias and oppression that Muslims face as a community and the growing insularity of the community due to external threats influence the decisions of minority women into not registering cases of domestic violence.

The communalisation of this criminal law has grave implications for minority women, as they are systematically pushed into a system of control by their families and the community. Communal politics and the economic marginalisation of the community reduce options for women, especially those trapped in violent situations.

Judicial interpretations: Domestic violence and women's roles

Judicial interpretations tend to support the accused in most cases of violence against women. While S498A gives an adequate definition of cruelty within marriage, encompassing physical and mental cruelty and including abetment to suicide, this provision has rarely been used except in case of grave physical injury or death, and primarily in dowry related cases of violence (Kapur 1993, 176). A survey conducted in rural Maharashtra revealed that most cases of domestic violence take between 3–5 years before a judgment is passed at the Sessions Court level, and that there are only 10 per cent convictions in cases of murders and 15 per cent in cases of attempted murders related to domestic violence (Seshu and Bhonsale nd, 24–7). In cases of domestic violence, cases are often filed under different sections of the IPC, which can sometimes work against the interests of the victim. In one case of suicide, the High Court found that the accused was not guilty of cruelty under S498A and

---

12   Verbal Presentation by Hasina Khan, Seminar on Fundamentalism and Women. Baroda. 16–18 October 1996.

consequentially he was not considered guilty under S304 (dowry death) (Shanti v. State of Haryana 1991, 1226).

It has also been argued that S 498A creates a situation of 'double jeopardy', that it replicates the provisions of S 4, Dowry Prohibition Act. Hence, the accused is tried twice for the same crime, which is legally untenable. This petition was rejected by Justice G R Luthra, who held that S 4, Dowry Prohibition Act punished the mere demand of dowry, even without accompanying cruelty and that S 498A was an aggravated form of that offence. Hence, a person could be prosecuted in respect of both offenses (Inder Raj Malik and Others v. Mrs. Sunita Malik 1986, 1510). What was not recognised even in this judgement was that S498A provides for punishing domestic cruelty unaccompanied with dowry demands, hence it does not in any case replicate the Dowry Prohibition Act.

Cases tried under S498A therefore reveal the judicial reluctance to convict men of domestic violence even when there appears adequate evidence. In a case of suicide tried by the Supreme Court, the accused was convicted for cruelty under S498A, not for abetment to suicide, in spite of an acknowledgement of cruelty, which could conceivably have been construed as abetment. The nature of cruelty, as accepted by the court was that repeated demands were made by the husband and parents-in-law for articles of dowry and money. As the judge pointed out:

> There is evidence that Veena made statements after her marriage and right up to the time when she died that she and her parents were being harassed by Wazir Chad, Kanwar Singh and his family members for dowry articles and also for money... In fact, what is the most telling circumstance is that after the death of Veena, a large number of dowry items seem to have been taken back by Veena's family members from Wazir Chad's residence, which were admittedly given as dowry. There is also substantial evidence to show that an amount of Rs. 20,000 to 25,000 was demanded from Krishan Kumar, the brother of Veena, and her mother... and they were unable to satisfy these demands (Wazir Chand v. State of Haryana 1989, 382)

Given these circumstances, it is somewhat difficult to comprehend why the accused was acquitted of the charge of abetment to suicide under S 306. Since harassment and cruelty were indeed proved beyond doubt in this case, it could conceivably lead to a situation wherein a young bride would find suicide the only option. However, the conviction under only S498A, not under S306 or both sections, benefited the accused, as the maximum punishment under S306 exceeds that prescribed for S498A.

The judiciary has, in other cases, used traditional arguments about the role of women to acquit violent and abusive husbands. In 1984, the Supreme Court set free Sharad Birdhichand Sarda, a Chemical Engineer, who had been found guilty of murdering his twenty-year-old wife, Manjushree Sarda, by suffocation and oral admission of potassium cyanide by the Sessions Court and the Bombay High Court. The SC acquitted Sarda, after studying the written DD by Manjushree Sarda, oral statements made by her parents, sister and friend about the ill-treatment meted out to her by her husband and his extra-marital relationship. The judgment reads as follows:

> Manjushree appears to be not only a highly sensitive woman, who expected whole-hearted love...from her husband, but having been thoroughly disappointed ...she may have chosen to end her life...A hard fact of life, which cannot be denied, is that some people, in view of their occupation or profession, find little time to devote to their family. Speaking in a lighter vein, lawyers, professors, doctors and perhaps judges, fall within this category, and to them, Manjushree's case should be an eye opener (Sharad Birdhichand Sarda v. State of Maharashtra 1984, 1622).

Therefore evidence of violence and betrayal by the husband was ignored by the judge to construct an image of an overly-sensitive woman, who made unreasonable demands of undivided attention from her busy husband. The case became a focal point for feminist groups in Mumbai who led protests against the judgment, including a poster exhibition, titled, 'Me Ek Manjushree' (I am Manjushree) and a signature campaign urging for a review petition into the case. The appeal, however, was rejected by the Supreme Court (Haksar and Singh 1986, 101).

In another case, it was ruled that even though cruelty was established, not every instance of harassment or every type of cruelty would attract prosecution under S498A. In a somewhat limited reading of the provision, it was suggested that 'it must be established that beating and harassment was with a view to force (the) wife to commit suicide or to fulfill illegal demands of (the) husband or in-laws' (Smt Sarla Prabhakar Wagmare v. State of Maharashtra and Others 1990, 407). By linking Sec.498A to death and dowry, the judge ignored the spirit of the law, which defines cruelty in much wider terms. In this as in other cases of violence, the judiciary appears to be influenced by 'conventional' patterns of wifely behavior. One reason for acquitting the accused was that the evidence of the woman was not considered consistent, because the woman had withdrawn police complaints of being burnt by her brother-in-law two months after her marriage, after when she returned to her natal home (Smt. Sarla Prabhakar Wagmare v. State of Maharashtra and Others, 408). This was seen as 'difficult to appreciate' (Smt Sarla Prabhakar Wagmare v. State of Maharashtra and Others, 408), therefore ignoring the centrality of marriage and the marital home, and appreciating potential pressure from the natal family to withdraw the case in order to preserve the marriage.

However, judges seem reluctant to punish men, even in cases of domestic violence where the guilt is clearly established. In a 1986 case, heard in the Punjab and Haryana High Court, it was ruled that the woman had indeed been burnt herself to death, following demands of dowry by the husband and rejected a petition that since the crime had taken place prior to the inclusion of S113A, IEA and S498A, the accused could not be punished under these sections. He ruled that, being a part of the rules of procedure, changes in Evidence Act, like in other rules of procedure are retrospective in nature. However, the sentence of the accused was reduced, even though guilt was established:

> Having viewed the case from all possible angles, I am of the view that the deceased did not die an accidental death, but rather committed suicide on account of the cruel conduct adopted by the appellant... and in this way, he abetted her suicide. (The) charge against the

appellant is this proved to the hilt. Accordingly, his conviction is maintained. His sentence of imprisonment is, however, reduced to four years rigorous imprisonment, while...taking into account the consumerism which has afflicted all sections of society, more particularly the lower middle classes and their race "to keep up with the Joneses" (1986 Cri L J 2092).

The judgment reflects simultaneously a synthetic concern for consumerism and an elitist upper class bias, which are used to absolve the murderer of individual responsibility for his crime.

It seems that the insertion of S113 IEA and Sec. 498A IPC did not seem to have improved the lot of women experiencing domestic violence, battered women, given that the judiciary has such 'stringent' methods to measure cruelty against women.[13] The rate of conviction in cases of domestic violence continues to be very low, and the law is invoked only in cases of grave physical violence, and mental cruelty is rarely accepted as legally valid in cases involving domestic violence, unless they are accompanied by physical violence.[14]

In contrast to the stringent standards adopted by the judiciary to cruelty by men, women are judged by totally different standards as far as what legally constitutes cruelty against husbands by wives. Under various civil marriage laws, including the Hindu Marriage Act, 1955, cruelty is a ground for divorce is cruelty, and can be used by either party. Cases decided under HMA 1955 judge cruelty in gender specific ways, therefore if a husband beats his wife occasionally, refuses to give her medical treatment as prescribed by the Doctor, takes alcohol and is indifferent to her health while she is pregnant, no case of cruelty is built up. However, in a 1984 case, it was ruled that if a wife undergoes a Medical Termination of Pregnancy without the consent of the husband, it amounted to cruelty, especially in the case of hindu families where sons have a ritual role to perform (cited in Menon 1995b, 369–392).

Clearly, in civil law, where mental cruelty is a ground for divorce, the ambiguity of the term is used to absolve men and to chastise women. Stringent rules of wifely behavior as set by the judge's perception of religious law and tradition are used to measure the rightness of women's actions, while neglect and physical violence by men are condoned.

To return to the provision of criminal law, there are some rare judgments that acknowledge the need to punish mental cruelty on men by women. A judgment by the Bombay High Court upheld a conviction by the Sessions Court, Pune, which had found the husband guilty of mental cruelty under S498 A. The husband had initiated

---

13   Prior to the insertion of S498A, the section often used for wife murders was S300 IPC, 1860, which states that culpable homicide is not murder, ' if the offender, whilst deprived of the power of self-control by grave and sudden provocation, causes the death of the person, who gave the provocation.' The test for provocation was that the provocation must have been sufficient to anger 'a reasonable man'.

14   In one case, where the wife had committed suicide since her husband was involved with another woman, the judge ruled that the act of the husband keeping a mistress was not an act that could provoke a woman to commit suicide, see Babu Shankar Jadhav v. State of Maharashtra. SC 172/88 cited in Seshu and Bhonsale nd, 48.

criminal proceedings against his wife and made allegations against her character. The wife had filed a complaint under Sec. 498A that this amounted to mental cruelty under S498A, The Sessions Court awarded the man six months imprisonment and a fine of Rs. 3000. On appeal, the Sessions Court set aside the imprisonment and doubled the fine. The wife appealed to the Bombay High Court on the grounds that the reduction of sentence amounted to a miscarriage of justice and rendered the judicial system suspect (cited in Agnes 1995, 115).

However, such judgments are extremely rare. However, in spite of such an abysmal record displayed by the police and the judiciary in cases of cruelty against married women, the overwhelming feeling displayed by the both sections is that this law is being 'misused' by women. In 1992, a retired public prosecutor stated that S498A was being misused by women, and the judiciary had problems with it (cited in Women's Centre 1994, 16). This view was reiterated in 1995 by Justice M L Phendse, Acting Chief Justice of the Bombay High Court at the valedictory function of a day long seminar on criminology held at the Bombay University Department of Law and the Greater Bombay Legal Advice Committee. He stated that his experience had revealed that in Maharashtra, the section on marital cruelty is misused by women to harass their husbands and in-laws. According to the judge, if the woman is burnt, she is tutored by her relatives to incriminate her husband's relatives, leading to their imprisonment. The judge went on to say:

> You can imagine the effect on the husband's family. When the police comes to the husband's doorstep, everyone feels he must be guilty...Life is much larger than law and sometimes, implementation of certain legislative provisions causes damage. Please examine whether these provisions have served the purpose of the legislature or cause damage to society (cited in *The Times of India* 1995).

Justice Phendse felt that wives commit suicide, not only due to harassment by their spouses or in laws, but because some women had a low level of tolerance, citing the example of a 19 year old married woman, who set herself on fire when chided by her husband for not keeping milk at home (cited in *The Times of India* 1995).

Phense's opinions have also been the basis of men's rights organisations in the country that suggest that domestic violence laws are being used maliciously by young married women against their aged in laws and innocent husbands (PSS 2005).

These arguments have been partially accepted by some women's movement activists, most notably, Delhi-based activist, Madhu Kishwar, who wrote in 1994 that since most women's groups are 'flooded with complaints of harassed wives, they have come to focus exclusively on women's problems as wives or daughters-in-law, rather than as daughters, sisters, mothers or grandmothers' (Kishwar 1994, 11), suggesting that the provision is misused by young women to harass their aged mothers-in-law, thereby reversing the harassment suffered traditionally by newly-married women by older women in the marital family, thereby believing that S498A like some other 'stringent laws such as TADA' (Kishwar 1994, 11) are being misused, and women's organisations are preferring to ignore this abuse.

While Kishwar's starting premise is valid, that the IWM has focused almost exclusively on violence against married women, not on the issues relating to single women, her conclusions are open to debate. To suggest that single women within the family are harassed by unscrupulous daughters-in-law merely inverts popular notions that most dowry deaths are initiated by mothers-in-law, ignoring power relations within Indian families where men enjoy power directly and women have access to fragments of power based on their relationships with men.[15] Kishwar's analysis – and Justice Phendse's – absolves men of all responsibility and guilt of perpetuating violence against women, placing it on women. In this understanding, women as wives are either foolish or self destructive enough to kill themselves on 'trivial' grounds or vindictive enough to throw out helpless old women out of their homes and to harass their husbands.

Perhaps the basis of this analysis is a sense of discomfort experienced when women are given rights within the family that conflict with patriarchal and familial rights, even though, as we have seen, these rights are ephemeral given the reluctance of the CJS to enter and follow up such cases. Some of this despair has been expressed in this letter written by some Bombay based feminists protesting the statements made by Justice Phendse:

> In view of the increasing number of murders, suicides, and sexual abuse of women both in public and in domestic spheres, and the increasing commodification of women's bodies in the media, we need to protest very seriously against each instance of judicial bias against women. Under such (an)...environment, we need to mobilise all our strength in order to protect the meagre legal provisions bestowed upon women... It appears that all the efforts of sensitising the judiciary and the state machinery regarding women's issues seem to have been in vain (FAOW 1995).

The Domestic Violence Act 2005 and conclusions

In 2005 the Indian state passed the Domestic Violence Act, 2005, that was closely aligned to the draft bill submitted by feminist organisations nationally in 2004. The Act is meant to

> ...protect the rights of women who are victims of violence of any kind occurring within domestic relationships, to prevent the victims from further domestic violence, to give effect to the provisions of the CEDAW and to provide for protection orders, residence orders, monetary relief and other matters referred to and for matters connected therewith or incidental thereto (Government of India 2005).

The new law recognises domestic violence to include physical, mental, emotional, financial and sexual abuse against women in domestic relationships. It offers women

---

15 Ironically Kishwar (1997) has made a convincing argument about the power and prestige enjoyed by older women in the family due to their status as mothers of sons, that allows them to oppress daughters-in-law.

rights currently unavailable to them in domestic violence situations, including right to matrimonial home, custody of children in domestic violence cases and compensation from the perpetrator. Influenced by arguments made by feminists including Kishwar, the law includes all women living in domestic relationships, including mothers-in-law and sisters-in-law, who could conceivably file cases of domestic violence against younger married women in the family. The latter provision has been opposed by some women's organisations nationally as potentially leading to men pressuring their mothers and sisters to file false cases against their wives (AIDWA 2004). However, this Act appears to see the issue of domestic violence as distinct from dowry related violence, which is an important legal shift in reconceptualising domestic violence.

While it is too early to assess the impact of this Act, what is significant here is that in spite of debates about the validity of law, and the lack of faith that some sections of the feminist movements have articulated, law continues to remain a significant arena of intervention for Indian feminists in the context of domestic violence. The larger debate on whether working with law is indeed a 'subversive' activity for feminists (Kapur and Cossman 1996), that has the potential for wider feminist transformation or following Menon (1995, 370) whether feminist engagements with law actually work against feminist ethics of emancipation by co-opting feminist issues within state and hegemonic discourses is a theme that we will keep coming back to in the book.

In the case of domestic violence activism, we have seen that that legal activism has yielded some 'benefits' for women including a redefinition of domestic violence from dowry related violence to mental and physical cruelty against married women to experiences of violence experienced by all women in domestic situations. The 2005 Act conceptualises domestic violence in terms of human rights debates. The study of legislative debates in the 1980s brings out the influence of feminist politics: during the debates on domestic violence, many of the demands of the women's movement were raised, and sometimes accepted by legislators.

Integration, however, remains largely partial, and feminists find that the laws both as conceptualised and implemented are inadequate, often token gestures to feminism. The implementation is dismal, belying even the limited gains that could have been made through these laws. The review of case law following the implementation of Section 498A reveals that not all women benefited from the new law; on the contrary, there have been few changes in judicial attitudes. Section 498A has been maligned as a law unfair to families, and of more consequence to feminists, unfair to single and older women in the family.

As we have seen, Indian feminists are not unaware of these issues and problems. At a general level, it is safe to postulate that most feminists have little or no faith in legal solutions to violence, but at the level of activism, see few viable alternatives other than the formal structure of law. For many feminists, therefore law remains a significant arena for feminist intervention, and the dreams of a feminist jurisprudence are not completely lost.

Chapter 7

Conclusions

This concluding chapter will bring together some of the themes discussed in the previous chapters. As the book has hopefully demonstrated, the Indian feminist movement is as strong, vibrant and polyvocal in 2006 as it has ever been, and many of the debates that have been raised in the book are both unresolved, and contested. Indian feminists have a sophisticated understanding of Indian society, patriarchy and law – simultaneously understanding its limitations and attempting to work within it, and with it. Therefore the conclusion (as indeed this book) offers a sympathetic 'critique from within' and points to the need to celebrate the diverse strengths of Indian feminist movements, and their ability to meet challenges from different quarters, that is, challenges from caste movements, communalism and globalisation. This final chapter will look at the debates on law within feminism: therefore what feminist responses have been to the contestation of law as a site for feminist activism; how feminists have worked to accommodate challenges from caste and community groups; and finally some of the strengths of the feminist movements and their contributions to new understandings of Indian sexualities, reconceptualising violent women within a broader comprehension of patriarchy and the ways in which western feminisms have both contributed to, and can learn from the creativity and courage of the Indian women's movements.

Campaigning for rights or cooption?

As we have seen throughout the book, the use of law and the rhetoric of rights by feminists has been a contested site for feminists in India. Some feminists have successfully appealed to the Indian State based on human rights, and women's rights, leading to legal amendments in several areas related to violence against women, including rape, sexual harassment in the workplace, representation of women, domestic violence and dowry. However, a critique has also been made of feminist reiteration of, and preoccupation with rights for women, that are restrictive, and often work against the interests of women.

   I suggest that feminist preoccupation with gender as the sole or primary category of activism, and indeed of oppression, is responsible for leading some feminists to ignore other categories of oppression, including caste, class and community (Shah 2006). As we have seen in Chapter 4, members of FAOW have approached female same sex relationship as intrinsically egalitarian, as 'there is (within them) no inequality' (FAOW1995: 7), therefore ignoring any potential areas of inequality in interpersonal relationships other than gender. Therefore differences in the areas of caste, class and age are ignored as potential sites for relational violence. Interestingly members of FAOW that are part of LBT groups such as LABIA extend the argument further to deny or at least reject the possibility of sexual assault within any same sex relationships (Shah 2006). This sits somewhat uneasily with earlier self portrayals of the same feminist group as influenced by a socialist feminist analysis while debating rape (as we have seen in Chapters 2 and 5) and the acknowledgement of differences between women within the context of religious personal law (Chapter 3). However, it does point to the shifts and contradictions within feminist conceptualisations on equality, and the need to strategise regarding which (in)equalities to forefront within political struggles. At another level, it is the feminist understanding of Indian women as universally oppressed and needing protection (Pathak and Sunder Rajan 1989) that forms the basis of appeals to the State to create new laws, or amend existing ones that work in favour of 'women's interests'; while somewhat confusingly feminists have also argued and acknowledged that 'women are not a collectivity' (Sen 2000, 54).

Some feminists have argued that there is an inherent contradiction in approaching the state for redressal of rights, since it increases the legitimacy of the Indian State, which is seen an inherently exploitative of human rights of the marginalised.

> The language of rights in fact affirms the power of the state to negotiate, intervene and co-opt the victim. Ironically, when today it is the state that has become the greatest violator of the rights of its people. And, these sets of rights can be reduced to a set of legal provisions that are based on the language of victimhood, not of survival, resistance and strength of communities who are being violated. (Asian Women's Human Rights Commission and Vimochana 1999, 8).

The reference here is to the role of the Indian State in perpetuating violence against women structurally by the implementation of laws that work against women's interests; by supporting and protecting the interests of those who perpetrate violence against women; and in the wider interests that the Indian State represents in terms of upper caste and Hindu ones, that work to marginalise working class and minoritised women. Therefore, while sections of the women's movements argue that the inclusion of feminist issues, and rhetoric into the concerns of the State is an achievement,[1] there is also a sense that this should be analysed as a cooption of feminist movements. For, it is feminist language that has been adopted, not the politics, and the language is used to enhance the image of the ruling political party. As an introspective piece by Mumbai based feminists puts it:

> There is a dichotomy in the way the Women's Movement interacts with the State. Many in the movement have looked at the state with suspicion, because it has played a major role

---

1   Based on interviews with Gopika Solanki, Social Worker, Special Cell to help Women and Children, Mumbai on 25 January 1999; and discussions with members from FAOW, Mumbai and Saheli, Delhi between 1997–99.

in the perpetuation of women's oppression. Yet, in its campaigns, the movement has ended up demanding legislative reforms. Why is it so? Is it because women perceive themselves as too weak to work towards alternatives? Or, is it that women actually perceive the state as an ally? (Gothoskar et. al. 1994, 3022).

As we have seen, state cooption of feminism has led to the creation of laws that could have long term negative consequences for women, therefore the creation of laws such as the 'custodial rape' provision in 1983 that shifted the onus of proof from the victim to the accused (Chapter 5) and the representation of women law in 1986 (Chapter 4) that increased the power of the State over private citizens has been analysed as creating a context where it was seen as acceptable that the human rights of the accused could be eroded. It has been suggested that this had led to a situation where human rights are in themselves threatened with consequences for religious minorities in the form of stringent anti terrorist laws (Gandhi 1989: 377–85). Feminists have therefore noted the entry of the State in to the realm of feminist language, while fulfilling anti feminist aims, for instance, it becomes difficult for feminists to respond 'when population planners invoke women's empowerment in their campaigns to introduce highly risky injectable female contraceptives and hormonal implants in India' (Tharu and Niranjana 1996, 138).

While the State's cooption of feminist rhetoric and politics has been acknowledged, there is a need to address the ways in which right wing Hindu fundamentalist parties and organisations have used feminism to the detriment of the interests of women, which can sometimes have consequences more widely for civil society and human rights. The issue of pornography is an obvious example. As we have seen in Chapter 4, the feminist campaign against pornography in the 1980s was highjacked by the members of Hindu right wing forces, who joined feminists in blackening posters. Similarly feminists have found that their statements opposing aspects of Muslim personal law on grounds of gender justice have quoted with approval by the BJP to create a negative image of Muslim law, based on communal principles (cited in Gangoli 1995, 22).

Therefore, political trends, that may be in practice anti feminist can and do articulate constructs of womanhood that may on the surface seem empowering. These include the diverse images thrown up by Saadhvi Rithambara, RSS ideologue, and Sushmita Sen, Miss Universe of Indian origin, both invoking the language of feminist politics with consummate ease. Saadhvi Rithambhara while promoting anti Muslim rhetoric and promoting sexual violence by Hindu men towards Muslim women, has been promoted as a 'fiery feminist' by the media; and Sushmita Sen, Miss Universe, considers herself a feminist while she is seen as symbol of increased consumerisation of the Indian economy and the commodification of Indian women (Kishwar 1995, 26–31). Their very glibness makes them more attractive as images of individual empowerment and strength than feminist imagery and activism that calls for collective action and struggle.

The issue of cooption can be analysed in another way. As we have seen in Chapter 4, feminist debates on sexuality not only draw upon the state for legitimacy, but also share with it some assumptions on female and male sexuality. Some of the debates on pornography bring out the moralism that is inherent in some sections of the movement. The ambivalence on homosexuality echoes socially constructed norms of sexual behavior. Chapter 5 reveals that some feminist debates on rape draw on socially and legally accepted parameters of sexual violations, while others attempt to challenge these. In addition, working within the law calls for strategic compromises to be made sometimes at the level of principles – as we have seen in the case of legal challenges posed by the bar dancers ban in Chapter 4, where the union distanced themselves from sex workers in order to increase their chances for a victory in the courts. While these are vexed issues for feminist activism, the diversity in views and the contestation of issues reveals a complexity within the Indian women's movement.

Reinterpreting tradition

Some feminists argue that by constantly appealing to the state, feminists have 'invoked the language of liberal secularism and citizenship' (Anveshi Law Team 1997, 435) which feeds into the representation of caste and community as being pre-modern and backward. As we have seen in Chapter 3, debates around the rights of minority women have been focused on contesting representations of minority communities, into which feminists have sometimes been complicit. It has therefore been suggested therefore that feminist prioritising of gender over caste-class-community has alienated women, as the notion of uniformity in law 'bypasses a whole network of relations within which women function' (Anveshi Law Team 1997, 435).

Critiques of coercive uniformity in law are valid, as there is enough evidence within Indian law to suggest that it can lead to violations of democratic norms, and women's rights. Therefore a construction of the 'ideal Hindu wife' within matrimonial law can marginalise single women from within and outside the community. Chapter 4 and 6 has revealed that there is a continuum within criminal and civil law in the way that women's sexuality is constructed, and that where laws are 'uniform' for all communities, as criminal laws are, they are seldom 'gender sensitive', as the debates on rape and domestic violence reveal. Within civil law, differential and multiple oppressions exist, while within criminal laws, oppression is uniform for women of different communities.

It has been suggested that one way out of the impasse is to re-interpret tradition in feminist ways, allowing women, allowing feminists to discover their roots in positive, pro women ways to prevent alienation from within the community (Menon 1994; Chaudhuri 2004). Therefore efforts have been made to understanding the ways in which women understand religion, and to find ways within religious or caste communities to combat patriarchy, as in the case of Delhi based Action India Women's Programme, which has worked on its initial programme of women's health within urban working class areas to create women's *panchayats* (local self governmental bodies) that deal with cases including domestic violence and sexual harassment. Therefore working class and Dalit feminists work with women in the community to challenge mainstream patriarchal constructions of female roles in the home or outside it. Similarly feminists from minority communities work with women from their communities to form an internal critique of minority law, and practice.

As we have seen, these efforts are challenged, as they are seen as appealing to 'primordial' concerns that are inherently non-feminist (Sangari 1995). The limitations of such critiques is that they choose to portray 'caste' and 'community' in somewhat rigid terms, seeing them as inherently unchanging, and totally impervious to change, which can be challenged by sympathetic re-readings of Indian history, that have pointed to the fluidity of these categories (for instance, see Sarkar 1985).

However, it can also be conversely argued that it might be somewhat short sighted to make a tacit equation between law and uniformity. Law is not a completely homogenising discourse, and in parts can acknowledge and enforce differences, as forms of affirmative action taken by the state reveal.[2] This is not of course, an effort to white wash the state, or state policy on gender or indeed to construct the State as a upholder of women's rights, but to make the limited point that like categories like gender, class, caste and community, the State vis-à-vis the legal arena is not homogeneous. As this book has consistently demonstrated in the context of legislative debates on rape (Chapter 5) and domestic violence (Chapter 6); and police and judicial responses to women experiencing violence, the various arms of the Indian State is demonstrably anti women. However, the experiences of women like Shahnaaz Shaikh and Shah Bano reveals that religious communities or caste groups can be equally misogynist, and may not necessarily open to feminist intervention. Women, like men, are formed through multiple identities, and to prioritise any one can perhaps strengthen hierarchies within that identity. Various castes and communities have oppressed women in multiple ways, while some have well have provided a space – sometimes limited – to women, just as law has. It can therefore be argued that Anveshi is doing to caste and community what Marxists have notoriously done to class, and some feminists to gender, that is to refuse to see any contradictions within that category of analysis.

In such a situation, to leave the legal arena unfought and unchallenged would be counter productive, and increase the alienation of women within the formal legal system. In addition, some feminists have argued that the language of citizenship and rights, restricted as it may well be, has provided Indian feminists a significant entry point into Indian politics. As citizens, women have a formal right to demand justice from the state, which is denied to them as members of their communities.[3] As we have seen in Chapter 3, this does pose the question of what happens to 'non citizens' – state sponsored atrocities on Bangladeshi men and women, forced repatriation of sex workers from Nepal – or 'quasi' citizens as in the case of minority women,

---

2   The proposal to reserve 33 per cent of seats for women in the legislature, and reservations of seats in *panchayats* is an obvious example of such affirmative action.

3   I owe this point to Uma Chakravarti, Working Group on Women's Rights, New Delhi.

who can be left out of the debates on rights based on citizenship. However, I would argue that in spite of the several limitations of the legal campaigns of the feminists in Bombay, and elsewhere, that the discourse of rights and citizenship has not completely lost its validity for feminist practice.

It has been suggested by some feminists that intrinsic to the critique of rights as invalid in the Indian context is a postmodern claim that truth and knowledge are contingent and multiple, therefore women cannot claim solidarity on the grounds of gender alone. Valuable as this insight is, and has been integrated for long into feminist politics and theory, when articulated as a critique of feminist practice by feminist practitioners themselves, it can be a potential cause for anxiety. Some feminist anthropologists have argued that feminist theories and post modernism can be wielded together in uneasy and problematic ways, to the detriment of the former. For, feminism is based on political action, post modernism is historically situated in the disillusionment, loss of control and mastery of hitherto socially dominant groups, i.e., white men. It has also been suggested that it is significant that post modern angst about truth claims have been made 'precisely when women and non western peoples have begun to speak for themselves, and indeed to speak of global systems of power differentials' (Lees et. al. 1986, 14–15). In other words, postmodern despair that truth does not exist or is unknowable may well be an inversion of western arrogance that allows only white men to define and articulate the 'truth'. When western white males have (through the assertion of women and non western people) lost the political power to define the truth, their response is that there is no truth to be discovered (Lees et. al. 1986, 15).

This critique of postmodernism however begs the question of why non western women and feminists articulate post modern claims, when it clearly does not benefit them. A critique of rights and legal intervention that goes beyond that of cooption and faulty implementation needs to be unpacked, and in the words of political theorist Neera Chandoke, the 'return to communitarianism' and the celebration of the 'local' (Chandoke 1997, 3321) within the Indian feminist movements needs to be contextualised as being influenced by the entrenchment of globalisation as an economical and social process. Chandoke suggests that globalisation, which marks the prising open of communities and national boundaries to the logic of market forces and capital creates 'overwhelming urge' for the longing for an often mythised community (Chandoke 1997, 3321). There is, however, a strong need to problematise the community, as feminists have done with the state, and to look at the status of women – and men – within the community. A larger question that emerges is: what are the ways in which the destructive potential of globalisation, both cultural and economic, can be opposed without celebrating the negative aspects of communities and caste groups.

I argue that the appeal to return to a mythised past is a part of the agenda of both the organised right in the context of the creation of a Hindutva state (Narula 2003), as of the some feminists, including but not confined to Dalit and minority feminists. The latter, however articulate their projections of the community in terms that are both critical of rightwing articulations, as well as looking at the ways in which feminist principles can be found within reinterpretations of the past, and projections of the future This includes feminist attempts to reinterpret Hindu culture creatively, therefore to recast Hindu goddesses such as Sita and Draupadi as quasi feminist figures, as well as to critique them through a feminist prism (Kishwar 1997; Dalmiya 2000) and attempts by Muslim feminists to reinterpret the Sharait to meet women's concerns (Ahmed 1995). The dilemma of possible collapse of positions with fundamentalist positions is a dilemma that needs to be addressed, along with the viability of such returns, even through feminist pasts.

Significantly debates on the validity of religious and cultural practices and traditions often do not challenge the denial of rights to minority Muslim women. In family courts, set up in the mid-1980s at the behest of the IWM to expedite civil matters pertaining to family laws, Muslim women have been kept out of the preview of the court. In other words, for matters including economic settlements, Muslim women have to go to the High Court, involving a process that is longer and more cumbersome than approaching the Family Courts. This is an issue that the women's movement has not taken up.

Abandoning law

While recognising the force of arguments that cast doubts on the validity and the ethics of feminist legal interventions, I have some reservations in accepting that legal reforms be abandoned by the IWM, and the focus be shifted exclusively, or even primarily on non legalist methods, which are considered less alienating. Since the IWM has always had an allegiance to multiple strategies, it seems somewhat limiting that one method of mobilisation and activism be abandoned completely. For many women abandoning law is an impossibility, and a reluctance to engage with the State a luxury that they cannot afford. For instance, Dalit and Muslim women and men are often confronted with the power of the State, especially the police, especially in the context of caste and community conflicts, and they are forced to challenge these forces, and need feminist support while doing so. Therefore, the legal arena remains significant both for feminist struggle, and for women, especially those who throng the courts in search of justice, even though it remains elusive, and at times illusionary.

Strengths within Indian feminisms

As is the nature of such works, including sympathetic critiques 'from within', this book has focused mostly on issues that the Indian feminist movements have failed to address, or have addressed in a somewhat problematic manner. However, the Indian feminism is one of the strongest movements in the world (see for instance: Gandhi and Shah 1989; International Initiative for Justice in Gujarat 2003; Eisenstein 2004), consistently posing since the late 1970s a challenge to Indian patriarchies, manifested within the Indian State, the family and civil society. It will therefore be fitting to end the book with a celebration of Indian feminism.

Challenges to sexuality

The women's movements campaigns have in the main, redefined sexuality in various significant ways, rejecting patriarchal and normative conceptualisations of female sexuality. As we have seen throughout the book, women identifying themselves as feminists – therefore understanding their positions as posing a challenge to patriarchal structures and institutions – are nevertheless divided in the ways they conceptualise their understanding of sexual difference. Therefore, streams within feminism have sometimes ignored aspects of female sexuality that they have felt uncomfortable with – therefore there has a feminist rejection of the 'vampish' or overtly sexualised images of women (Ghosh 1996; Gangoli 2005), or an acceptance of heterosexual and marital monogamy as being beneficial to women, and therefore desirable. Therefore, as we have seen in Chapter 3 and 4, some feminists base their opposition to legalisation of prostitution simultaneously on a rejection of non-monogamy as a possibility – both for men and for women – and a celebration of marriage as the only route for sexual satisfaction:

> From a feminist point of view, the proposal to legalise prostitution is untenable – why should it be assumed that men have certain urges which need an outlet urgently...The socialisation route is the route to take, so that young men are socialised to monogamy and young women are socialised to view sex as a beautiful, natural activity (so that they do not refuse sex to husbands after 2 or 3 children) not the legalisation route (Sanlaap 1998, 53–54).

As I have examined elsewhere (Gangoli 2000; Gangoli 2006), this view legitimises patriarchal notions of the family and monogamy by using quasi-feminist arguments, and appropriates feminism, speaking on behalf of all feminists. It also restricts sexuality to marital sexuality, allowing no space for women and men outside it to articulate their understanding of sexuality.

However, other feminists have questioned the normative nature of Indian heterosexuality, which is based on a celebration of sex within marriage, and a rejection of any form of non-marital sex. Therefore as we have seen in Chapter 4, appropriation from communal right wing forces of the campaign on pornography have pushed some Indian feminists to reconsider their positions on the campaigns on sexuality, moving them towards an opposition of non-sexual, discriminatory representations of women within the media. Others have continued to focus on degrading sexualised images of women, as ways to understand how patriarchy constructs women's bodies, while not advocating censorship (Gandhi and Shah 1989). Therefore some feminists have displayed an immense capacity for self-reflection and for change, and the ability therein to focus on the 'unconscious' and unstated assumptions of feminist politics, and rhetoric.

Chapters 4 and 5 therefore analyse the challenges made by women's movement campaigns to ideas of compulsory marriage, compulsory heterosexuality and the 'good' versus the 'bad' woman. Activists that are part of the LBT movement have challenged specifically the heterosexual orientation of some feminists, and have created a context wherein debates on the validity of laws criminalising male homosexuality create discussions on the mainstreaming of heterosexual relationships and their impact on women's lives. Similarly, Chapter 3, 5 and 6 reveal that feminist campaigns against rape and domestic violence dispute the notions of family and community 'honour' and 'shame' being vested in the body of the woman; and therefore reconceptualise 'shame' as belonging to the perpetrator of violence, rather than the victim. Therefore feminist activism in individual cases of rape and domestic violence work to 'shame' perpetrators by using 'traditional' practices such as blackening the faces of the men committing the crime, that have been used to dishonour women who have transgressed social norms.

Understanding the violent woman

As we have seen in the context of communal riots (Chapter 3), and domestic violence (Chapter 6), Indian feminists have had to acknowledge the nature of female violence against women as a part of Indian social structures. While mainstream debates on domestic violence often understand this in terms of women's essential lack of solidarity with other women, therefore popular projections of 'women are women's worst enemies' are seen as 'explaining' mother in law violence against daughters in law, Indian feminists have conceptualised it within a wider understanding of, and critique of patriarchy (Chapter 6). The power dynamics within the normative Hindu joint family, where older women with sons enjoy a dominant role within the family has been noted (Bumiller 1990; Kishwar 1997, Talwar-Oldenburg 2002), and feminists have analysed this precise power imbalance between women within the family as feeding into, and legitimising patriarchy.[4] While older women are often perpetrators of physical and emotional violence against younger women in the family, the power of the older woman is based on her relationships within the family, and she works therefore as a 'carrier of culture' (Yuval-Davis, 1997), therefore 'training' young married women into accepting their inferior position within the household.

As noted in Chapter 3, women conforming to patriarchal norms of sexual behaviour, sexual division of labour, and appearance are rewarded within the Indian context, while those transgressing them face reprisals, which other women often perpetuate. It is therefore an understanding of their own inferior and vulnerable position as women, and the potential oppression that younger women and girls can face within the family and community that can therefore influence women's decisions to participate in, and sometimes initiate female infanticide and sex selective abortions (Gangoli 1998a) and explain the often rigid sexual control that is often exercised on single women and young girls by their mothers. In this context, the actions of mothers in training their daughters into normative and acceptable sexual and social behaviours can be understood as a way of offering some future protection against patriarchies, rather than an act of woman-hating. On the contrary, mother in law initiated violence against daughters in law and female infanticide can be seen as

---

4   Based on discussions with members of Forum Against Oppression of Women.

an act of self-preservation – the woman maintaining her superior position within the family as a real or potential mother of sons.

As elaborated in Chapter 3, some Hindu women have initiated, or colluded with violence against minority women and men during communal conflicts (International Initiative for Justice in Gujarat 2003). While this contradicts constructions of women being primarily victims of sexual violence during conflict and therefore as essentially against war and conflict (Das 1995; Menon and Bhasin 1998); following events in Gujarat, feminists have argued that it is necessary to understand, and explain the role that women have played in perpetuating violence against women in communal riots (International Initiative for Justice in Gujarat 2003). As we have seen, within the family younger women are socialised – often violently – into proper female behaviour by their mothers and mothers in law; and women transgressing these roles are often the recipients of violence, both from men and women in the family or the wider community. During times of conflict, the focus often shifts to the woman from the 'enemy' camp, who is objectified in sexually explicit terms as desirable (Nussbaum 2004). Therefore, Hindu women were now called upon to maintain the patriarchy, and to demonstrate their allegiance to their community by encouraging men from their own community into perpetuating acts of violence, or by committing acts of violence themselves. Within the Muslim communities, we have seen that women experiencing the violence are often silenced by other women within the community from speaking out against the violence, as potentially dishonouring the family, and the extended community.

Influences from the west and influencing the west

While we began the book by addressing the ways in which Indian feminisms have been influenced by western feminisms, and how they have often had to respond to being 'westernised' as an accusation that needed addressing, it may be fitting to end the book by looking at some of the many lessons that western feminists could potentially learn from Indian feminisms.

As we have seen through the book Indian feminists have had a complex relationship with other social movements, including communist parties, trade unions, Dalit, gay rights, prostitute rights and environmental movements. There have been moments of conflicts, for instance left-wing parties accusing feminists of dividing the class struggle and feminists accusing leftist parties and trade unions as constructing the working class in hegemonic male orientated terms, and ignoring the rights of women, and in some cases colluding with male violence against women, where perpetrators are from within their political parties.[5]

However, in the main, feminists have worked with women and men from varied social movements, and have attempted to address and integrate the concerns of these

---

5   While I have attempted to discuss these issues consistently through the book, see especially Chapter 2 and Chapter 5 for debates on the differences within left-wing and feminist concerns.

movements in their own perceptions, and actions. Therefore autonomous feminists have supported and participated in trade union and workers' struggles in Mumbai; gay rights movements and anti communalisation movements, and feminists from mainstream left-wing parties have worked with autonomous feminists to oppose violence against women in its varied forms. In contrast, western feminist movements have often been characterised by their separatist politics (Dworkin 1983; Mackinnon 1993); and the ability of Indian feminists to work with, while disagreeing with, aspects of the ideologies of other social movements could be potentially useful, and worthy of consideration by western feminists. In addition, as we have seen, Indian feminists have also contributed to increased understanding of the ways in which female violence against women can be seen as feeding into patriarchal control of women. Finally, while Indian feminists may not have resolved the issue of the role of legal intervention within feminist intervention they have contributed immensely to local, national and international debates on the issue.

Bibliography

A. Books, journal articles, book chapters and newspaper articles

'Saffron Brigade', *Frontline.* 6 January 1993.

'Women May Misuse Legal Loopholes: Phendse', *The Times of India,* 1 April 1995.

Abraham, A. (1991), 'Case Studies from the Women's Centre, Bombay', in Maitreyi Krishna Raj (ed.), *Women and Violence. A Country Report.* (Bombay, UNESCO), 60–65.

Abraham, A. (1992), 'A Legal Remedy for Harassed Wives?, *The Hindu*, 22 November 1992.

Agarwal, B. (1994), *A Field of One's Own: Gender and Land Rights in South Asia* (Cambridge: Cambridge University Press).

Agnes, F. (1988), 'Violence in the Family: Wife Beating' in Rehana Ghadially (ed.), *Women in Indian Society. A Reader* (New Delhi: Sage Publications), 163–180.

Agnes, F. (1990), *My Story...Our Story of Rebuilding Broken Lives* (Bombay: Majlis).

Agnes, F. (1992), 'Protecting Women Against Violence: Review of a Decade of Legislation, 1980–89', *Economic and Political Weekly* 27:17, ws 19–33.

Agnes, F. (1992), *Give Us This Day Our Daily Bread. Procedures and Case Laws on Maintenance* (Bombay: Majlis).

Agnes, F. (1993), 'The Anti-Rape Campaign: The Struggle and the Setback', in Chhaya Datar (ed.), *Violence Against Women* (Calcutta: Stree), 111–112.

Agnes, F. (1995), *State, Gender and the Rhetoric of State Reform. Gender and Law: Book 2* (Bombay: RCWS, SNDT).

Agnes, F. (1995), 'Hindu Men, Monogamy and Uniform Civil Code', *Economic and Political Weekly* 30:50, 3238–3242.

Ahmed L. (1995), 'Women and Gender in Islam: Historical Roots of a Modern Debate', *Iranian Journal of International Affairs* 7: 3, 706.

Ahmed-Ghosh, H. (2003), 'Writing the Nation on the Beauty Queen's Body Implications for a "Hindu" Nation', *Meridians: feminism, race, transnationalism,* 4:1, 205–227.

Anklesarwar Aiyer S. (1987), 'Women and the Law. Anti-Obscenity Bill Still Hangs Fire', *Indian Express,* 1 July 1987.

Anveshi Law Team (1997), 'Position Paper on Gender Just Laws', *Economic and Political Weekly* 32: 9, 453–458.

Babu, S. (1995), 'Emergency Remembered. The Intrinsic Value of Democracy', *The Times of India*, 20 June 1995.

Ballhatchet, K. (1980), *Race, Sex and Class Under the Raj. Imperial Attitudes and Policies and their Critics. 1793–1908* (London: Weidenfeld and Nicholson).

Baviskar, A. (1995), *In the Belly of the River. Tribal Conflicts over Development in the Narmada Valley* (New Delhi: Oxford University Press).

Baxi, P. (1995), *The Normal and the Pathological in the Construction of Rape. A Sociological Analysis* (M.Phil Thesis, Delhi: Department of Sociology, Delhi School of Economics, University of Delhi).

Baxi, P. (2001), 'Sexual harassment', *Seminar*, 505, http://www.india-seminar.com/2001/505/505%20pratiksha%20baxi.htm.

Baxi, U. (1994), *Inhuman Wrongs and Human Rights. Unconventional Essays* (New Delhi: Haranand Publications).

Bhargava, G.S. (1983), 'Towards a Common Civil Code', *Mainstream,* 22:9, 1983.

Brownmiller, S. (1993 edition), *Against our Will. Men, Women and Rape* (New York: Ballantine Books).

Bumiller, E. (1990), *May you be the mother of a hundred sons* (New York: Random House).

Butalia, U. (2000), *The Other Side of Silence: Voices from the Partition of India* (Durham: Duke University Press).

Chakravarti U. and Wahi, T. (1995), 'Recent Gender Crimes in the University of Delhi: Two Case Studies', *Revolutionary Democracy* 1:2, available online at: http://www.revolutionarydemocracy.org/rdv1n2/gender.htm.

Chakravarti, U. (1998) *Rewriting History, the Life and Times of Pandita Ramabai* (New Delhi: Kali for Women).

Chandoke, N. (1997), 'Communitarianism with Vengeance', *Economic and Political Weekly* 32:52, 3321–22.

Chudhuri, M. (ed.) (2004), *Feminism in India* (New Delhi: Kali for Women).

DeCunha, J. (1991), *The Legalisation of Prostitution. A Sociological Inquiry into the Laws Relating to Prostitution in India and the West* (Bangalore: Wordmakers).

Dalmiya V. (2000), 'Loving Paradoxes: A Feminist Reinterpretation of the Goddess Kali', *Hypatia-Edwardsville* 15:1, 125–150.

Das, V. (1995), *Critical Events* (New Delhi: Oxford University Press).

Das, V. (1996), 'Sexual Violence, Discursive Formations and the State', *Economic and Political Weekly* 31: 35–37, 2411–2423.

Datar, C. (1988), 'Reflections on the Anti-Rape Campaign in Bombay' in Saskia Witringa (ed.), *Women's Struggles and Strategies* (Aldershot: Gower Publications), 13–30.

Devi, R. (1993), 'Status of Women in India: A Comparison by State', *Asia-Pacific Population Journal* 8:4, 59–77.

Dhagamwar, V. (1989), *Towards a Uniform Civil Code* (New Delhi: Indian Law Institute).

Dhagamwar, V. (1992), *Law, Power and Justice. The Protection of Personal Rights in the Indian Penal Code* (New Delhi: Sage).

Dietrich, G. (1992) *Reflections on the Women's Movement in India: Religion and Development* (New Delhi: Horizon).

Dworkin, A. (1981), *Pornography: Men Possessing Women* (London: Women's Press).

Dworkin, A. (1983), *Intercourse* (New York: The Free Press).

Eisenstein, Z. (2004), *Against Empire: Feminisms, race and fictions of 'the' West* (London: Zed Books).

Eisentein Z. (1983), *The Radical Future of Liberal Feminism* (Boston: North East University Press).

Engineer, A. A. (ed.) (1987), *The Shah Bano Controversy* (Hyderabad: Orient Longman).

Farooqi, V. (1984), 'A Woman Destroyed. An Interview with Rameezabee', in Madhu Kishwar and Ruth Vanita (ed.), *In Search of Answers. Indian Women's Voices from Manushi* (London: Zed Books), 186–88.

Fruzzetti, L. (1982), *The Gift of a Virgin: Women, Marriage Ritual and Kinship in Bengali Society* (Piscataway, NJ: Rutgers University Press).

Fuller C.J. (ed.) (1997), *Caste Today* (New Delhi: Oxford University Press).

Gandhi, N. (1989), 'The Indecent Representation of Women (Prohibition) Act, 1986', *The Indian Journal of Social Work* 5:3, 377–85.

Gandhi, N. (1996), *When the Rolling Pin Hits the Streets. Women in the Anti-Price Movement in Maharashtra* (New Delhi: Kali for Women).

Gandhi, N. and Shah, N. (1989), *The Issues at Stake. Theory and Practice in the Contemporary Women's Movement in India* (New Delhi: Kali for Women).

Gangoli G. and Solanki, G. (1996), 'Misplaced Myths', *Humanscape* 3:4, 22–6.

Gangoli, G (1999) 'Reproduction, Abortion and Women's Health', *Social Scientist,* 28:11–12, 83–105.

Gangoli, G (2001). Prostitution as Livelihood: 'Work' or 'Crime', Available online at: http://www.anthrobase.com/Txt/G/Gangoli_G_01.htm#entry.

Gangoli, G. (2006), 'Sex Work, Poverty and Migration in Eastern India', in Sadhna Arya and Anupama Roy (eds.) *Poverty, Gender and Migration* (New Delhi: Sage), 214–36.

Gangoli, G. (1992), Gender relations in the cotton mill industry in Bombay, 1900–1993 (M.Phil thesis, Delhi: Department of History, University of Delhi).

Gangoli, G. (1995), *The Law on Trial: the Uniform Civil Code Controversy* (Bombay: Akshara Resource Centre).

Gangoli, G. (1997), *Report on Workshop on Domestic Violence and Muslim Women* (Bombay: Women Living Under Muslim Law).

Gangoli, G. (1998a), 'Reproduction, Abortion and Women's Health', *Social Scientist*, 28: 11–12, 83–105.

Gangoli, G. (1998b), 'The Right to Protection from Sexual Assault: the Indian anti-rape campaign', in Firoz Manji and Deborah Eade (eds.) *Development and Rights. Selected Essays from Development in Practice* (Oxford: Oxfam), 128–136.

Gangoli, G. (2000), *Silence Hurt and Choice: Attitudes to prostitution in India and the West* (London School of Economics, WP6).

Gellner E. (1995), 'The importance of being modular', in John Hall (ed.) *Civil Society: Theory, History, Comparison* (Cambridge: Blackwell).

Ghosh, S. (1996), 'Deviant pleasures and disorderly women. The representation of the female outlaw in Bandit Queen and Anjaam' in Ratna Kapur (ed.) *Feminist Terrains in Legal Domains. Interdisciplinary Essays in Women and Law in India* (New Delhi: Kali for Women), 150–183.

Gothoskar, S. et. al. (1994), 'Maharashtra's Policy for Women', *Economic and Political Weekly* 29, 3019–22.

Government of India (1965), *Jawaharlal Nehru, Speeches, 1949–53, Volume II* (New Delhi: Publications Divisions. Ministry of Information and Broadcasting).

Government of India (1984), 'On Proclamation of Emergency. Broadcast to the Nation. All India Radio. New Delhi. June 26, 1975', in *Selected Speeches and Writings of Indira Gandhi, Vol. III* (New Delhi: Publications Divisions. Ministry of Information and Broadcasting).

Gupta, V. (1991) 'Women Workers in Trade Unions', *Yojana* 11, 2.

Hague, G. and Malos, E. (1998, 2nd edition), *Domestic Violence: Action for Change* (Cheltenham: New Clarion Press).

Hague, G. et. al. (2003), *Is anyone listening? Accountability and Women Survivors of Domestic Violence* (London: Routledge).

Haksar, N. and Singh, A. (1986), *Demystification of Laws for Women* (New Delhi: Lancer).

Hasan, Z. (1998), 'Gender Politics, Legal Reform and the Muslim Community in India' in Patricia Jeffery and Amrita Basu (eds.) *Appropriating Gender: Politicization of Religion in South Asia* (New York: Routledge) 71–89.

Hensmen, R. (1987), *Oppression Within Oppression. The Dilemma of Muslim Women in India* (Mumbai: Women's Research and Action Group, Working Paper 1).

Hess, L. (1999), 'Rejecting Sita: Indian Responses to the Ideal Man's Cruel Treatment of His Ideal Wife', *Journal of the American Academy of Religions* 67:1, 1–30.

Human Rights Watch (1995), *Rape for Profit. Trafficking of Nepali Girls and Women to India's Brothels* (Human Rights Watch) http://www.hrw.org/reports/1995/India.htm.

Human Rights Watch (2001), *India Human Rights Press Backgrounder. Anti-Terrorism Legislation*, http://www.hrw.org/backgrounder/asia/india-bck1121.htm.

Human Rights Watch (2004), US Country Reports on Human Rights Practices in India, http://www.state.gov/g/drl/rls/hrrpt/2005/61707.htm.

India Centre for Human Rights and Law (1999), *Humjinsi – A Resource Book on Lesbian, Gay and Bisexual Rights in India* (Bombay: ICHRL).

Jaget, C. (ed.) (1980), *Our Lives* (Bristol: Falling Wall Press).

Jaisingh, I (1989) 'The Ignoble Servility of Pati Parmeshwar', *The Lawyers*, December 1989, 6.

Jayawardena, K. and de Alwis, M. (1996), *Embodied Violence: Communalizing Women's Sexuality in South Asia* (London and New Jersey: Zed Books).

John, M.E. (1996), *Discrepant Dislocations. Feminism, Theory and Post-Colonial Histories* (Berkeley: University of California Press).

Jones, A. (ed.) (2004*). Gender and Genocide* (Nashville: Vanderbilt University Press).

Kakar, S. (1995), *The Colours of Violence* (New Delhi: Viking, Penguin Books India).

Kannabiran, K. (1996), 'Challenge of Communalism' in Madhushree Datta, Flavia Agnes and Neera Adarkar (eds.), *The Nation State and Indian Identity* (Calcutta: Samya), 113–121.

Kapur, R. (1993), 'R v. Ahluvalia: The Vindication of Battered Women', *National Law School Journal* 1:1, 176.

Kapur, R. (1993), *Introduction on the Proposed Law on Sexual Assault* (New Delhi: Saakshi).

Kapur, R. (1996), 'Who Draws the Line? Feminist Reflections on Speech and Censorship', *Economic and Political Weekly* 31: 16–17, WS15–30.

Kapur, R. (2000), 'Too Hot to Handle: The Cultural Politics of Fire', *Feminist Review* 64, 53–64.

Kapur, R. and Cossman B. (1996), *Subversive Sites. Feminist Engagements with Law in India* (New Delhi: Sage).

Kapur, R. (1993), 'Case Comments: Rape, Challenging the Pedestals of Patriarchy', *National Law School Journal* 1:1, 168–171.

Karandikar, M.A. (1987), *Islam in India's Transition to Modernity* (New Delhi: Orient Longman).

Kishor, S and Gupta, K. (2004), 'Women's Empowerment in India and its States. Evidence from the NFHS', *Economic and Political Weekly* 39:7, 649–712.

Kishwar M. and Vanita, M. (1988), 'Axed', *The Illustrated Weekly of India*, August 7, 1988: 38–39.

Kishwar, M. (1994) 'Co-ownership Rights for Wives. A Solution Worse than the Problem', *Manushi* 84, 8–12.

Kishwar, M. (1994), 'Codified Hindu Law. Myth and Reality', *Economic and Political Weekly,* 29: 33, 2145–61.

Kishwar, M. (1995), 'When India "Missed" the Universe', *Manushi*, 88, 26–31.

Kishwar, M. and Vanita, R. (ed.) (1984), *In Search of Answers. Indian Women's Voices from Manushi* (London: Zed Books).

Kishwar, M. (1997), 'Women, Sex and Marriage. Restraint as a Feminine Strategy', *Manushi* 99, 23–36.

Koonz, C. (1987), *Mothers in the Fatherland. Women, the Family and Nazi Politics* (New York: St Martin's Griffins).

Kothari, R. (1995), 'Emergency Remembered. Positive and Negative Legacy', *The Times of India,* 23 June 1995.

Krishna Raj M. (1986), 'Reflections on Women and the Industrial Working Class Movement', *RCWS Newsletter,* December 1986, 9–10.

Kumari, J. and Kelkar, G. (1995), 'The Left and Feminism', *Economic and Political Weekly,* 24:38, 2123–6.

Kumari, R. (1989), *Brides are not for burning: Dowry Victims in India (*Delhi: Radiant Publishers).

Lateef, S. (1994), *Muslim Women in India. Political and Private Realities* (New Delhi: Kali for Women).

Lawyers Collective (1992), *Domestic Violence, Legal Aid Handbook I* (New Delhi: Kali for Women).

Lees, F. et. al. (1989), 'The Post Modern Turn in Anthropology. Cautions From a Feminist Perspective', Signs. *Journal of Women in Culture and Society* 40:1, 7–33.

Lees, S. (1996), *Carnal Knowledge? Rape on Trial.* (London: Hamish Hamilton).

Mackinnon, C. (1989), *Towards a Feminist Theory of the State* (Cambridge, Massachusetts: Harvard University Press).

Mackinnon, C.A. (1993), *Only Words* (Cambridge, Massachusetts:Harvard University Press).

Mani, L. (1998), *Contentious Traditions: The Debate on Sati in Colonial India* (Beverly: University of California Press).

Menon, N. (1995a), 'Destabilizing Feminism', *Seminar* 437, 100–103.

Menon, N. (1995b), 'The Impossibility of "Justice": Female Feoticide and Feminist Discourse on Abortion', *Contributions to Indian Sociology,* 29:1–2, 369–392.

Menon, N. (2004), *Recovering Subversion: Feminist Politics Beyond the Law* (New Delhi: Permanent Black).

Menon, R. (1994), 'The Personal and the Political' in Kamala Bhasin et. al. (eds.). *Against All Odds* (New Delhi: Kali for Women), 173–182.

Menon, R. and Bhasin, K. (1998), *Borders and Boundaries: Women in India's Partition* (New Delhi: Kali for Women).

Mikhail, S. B. L. (2002), 'Child marriage and child prostitution: two forms of sexual exploitation', *Gender and Development* 10:1, 43–49.

Multiple Action Research Group (1992), *Hamare Kanoon, Vol. IV* (New Delhi: MARG).

Multiple Action Research Group (1992), *Humare Kanoon, Volume V* (New Delhi: Women and Child Development, Human Resource Ministry).

Nandy, A. (1988), *Return from Exile* (New Delhi: Oxford University Press).

Narula, S. (2003), 'Overlooked Danger: The Security and Rights Implications of Hindu Nationalism in India', *Harvard Human Rights Journal* 16. 41–68.

Nussbaum, M.C. (2004), 'Body of the Nation. Why women were mutilated in Gujarat', *Boston Review* 29:3, available online at: http://bostonreview.net/BR29.3/nussbaum.html, accessed on 2/08/2004.

Omvedt, G. (1980), *We will Smash This Prison. Indian Women in Struggle* (London: Zed Publishers).

Pai Panandikar V.A. et. al. (1978), *Family Planning Under the Emergency* (New Delhi: Radiant Publishers).

Palkhiwala, N.A. (1995), Emergency Remembered. Preserving Constitution's Integrity, *The Times of India,* 26 June 1995.

Pandey, B. et al. (2003), *Trafficking in Women in Orissa* (Bhubaneswar: ISED, UNIFEM and USAID).

Panicker, L. (1995), 'Emergency's Shadow on Family Planning', *The Times of India*, 22 June 1995.

Patel, V. (1994), 'Sexual Harassment by the Police: Madhushree Datta' in Mira Kosambi (ed.), *Women's Oppression in the Public Gaze* (Bombay: RCWS, SNDT University), 107–119.

Pathak, Z and Sunder Rajan, R. (1989), 'Shah Bano', *Signs: Journal of Women in Culture and Society* 14:3, 558–582.

PUDR (1989), *Inside The Family* (New Delhi: PUDR).

PUDR (1994), *Custodial Rape* (New Delhi: PUDR).

Purao, P. and Savara, M. (1983), *Courage in Living* (Bombay: Annapurna Mahila Mandal).

Purewal J. and Kapur, N. (nd.), *Have You Been Sexually Assaulted?* (New Delhi: Norad).

Rai, S. M. (1995), 'Women and Public Power: Women in the Indian Parliament', *IDS Bulletin* 26:3, 86–93.

Rao, A. (2003), 'Indian feminism and the patriarchy of caste', *Himal* http://www.himalmag.com/2003/february/analysis_1.html.

Rao, P. (1982), *Marriage, The Family and Women in India* (New Delhi: Printox, South Asia Books).

Ray, R and Korteweg, A.C. (1999), 'Women's Movements in the Third World: Identity, Mobilisation and Autonomy', *Annual Review of Sociology*, 25, 47–71.

Raymond, N. (2003), 'Analysis of the bill to prevent sexual harassment of women in the workplace', *Combat Law,* available online at: http://www.pucl.org/Topics/Gender/2005/harassment.htm

Rohini P. H et. al. (nd.), *"My Life is one Long Struggle." Women, Work, Organisation and Struggle* (Belgaum: Pratishabd).

Rudd, J. (2001), 'Dowry Murders. An example of violence against women', *Women's Studies International Forum,* 24:5, 513–532.

Rushdie, S. (1991), *Imaginary Homelands. Essays and Criticism 1981–1991* (London: Granta Books).

SAARC (1998), The Declaration of the Ninth SAARC Summit in the Section, Women in Development (Male: SAARC).

Sahay, K.B. (1993), Snip out the Problem, *The Telegraph*, 19 January 1996.

Sangari, K. (1995), 'Politics of Diversity. Religious Communities and Multiple Patriarchies', *Economic and Political Weekly* 30:51, 3787–3810.

Sarkar, L. (1994), 'Rape: a human rights versus a patriarchal interpretation', *Indian Journal of Gender Studies,* 1:1, 69–72.

Sarkar, S. (1995), *Modern India* (New Delhi: Macmillan).

Sarkar, T. (1991), 'Reflections on Birati Rape Cases. Gender Ideology in Bengal', *Economic and Political Weekly*, 26 5, 215–218.

Schechter, S. (1982), *Women and Male Violence: The Visions and Struggles of the Battered Women's Movement* (London: Pluto).

Sen, A. (1998), 'Radical Needs and Moderate Reforms' in Jean Dréze and Amartya Sen (eds.) *Indian Development. Selected Regional Perspectives* (New Delhi: Oxford University Press), 1–28.

Sen, S. (2000), *Towards a Feminist Politics? The Indian Women's Movement in Historical Perspective* (The World Bank: Development Research Group/Poverty Reduction and Economic Management Network, Policy Research Report on Gender and Development, Working Paper Series No. 9).

Seshu, G. (2005), 'Nikaahnama: time for a gender-just model', *Humanscape* 12:4, 1–4.

Seshu, M. and Bhonsale, V. (nd), *Imprisoning Womanhood. A Report on the Desertions and Deaths of Women in Sanghli District* (Sanghli: VAMPS).

Shah Bano (1985), 'Open Letter to Muslims', *Inquillab*, 13 November 1985 (Translated from Urdu).

Shah, S. (1988), 'Taking a Look at Pornography', *Imprint*, June 1988: 42–48.

Singh, K. (1993), 'Women's Rights and the Reform of Personal Laws' in Gyanendra Pandey (ed.), *Hindus and Others. The Question of Identity in India Today* (New Delhi: Viking, Penguin Books India), 177–197.

Sinha, I. (1996), 'Report of the World Congress against Commercial Sexual Exploitation of Children, Stockholm in August 1996', *Jonaki. The Glow Worm* 1:1, 3–6.

Srivastava, K. and Ghosh, S. (1996), 'Against Our Will', *Humanscape* 3:4, 20–21.

Sunder Rajan, R. (2003), *The Scandal of the State. Women, Law and Citizenship in Postcolonial India*, (New Delhi: Permanent Black).

Talwar Oldenburg, V. (2002), *Dowry murder. The imperial origins of a cultural crime* (New Delhi: Oxford University Press).

United Nations (1998), *Women and HIV/AIDS Concerns – a focus on Thailand, Philippines, India and Nepal.* Available online at: http://www.un.org/womenwatch/daw/csw/hiv.htm

van der Hootge, L. and Kingma, K. (2004), 'Providing cultural diversity and the rights of women: the dilemmas of "intersectionality" for development organisations', *Gender and Development,* 12:1, 47–55.

Varney A. (2002), *Ethnic Conflict and Civic Life* (New Haven and London: Yale University Press).

Vibhuti et. al. (1983), 'The Anti-Rape Movement in India', in Miranda Davis (ed.), *Third World, Second Sex: Women's Struggles and National Liberation* (London: Zed Books), 180–90.

Wijer, M. and Lin, L.C. (1997), *Trafficking in women. Forced Labour and Slavery Like Practices* (The Netherlands: Foundation Against Trafficking in Women and GAATW).

Women's Centre (1994), *Towards Survival and Empowerment. Report of the Women's Centre. 1991–1994* (Bombay: Women's Centre).

Working Group for Women's Rights (1996), Statement on Uniform Civil Code. A Debate, *Alternatives/ Vikalp* 5:3, 90–91.

Yllo, K., and Bograd, M. (eds.) (1988), *Feminist perspectives on wife abuse* (Newbury Park, CA: Sage).

Yuval-Davis, N. (1997), *Gender and Nation* (London: Sage).

Yuval-Davis, N. and Anthias, F. (eds.) (1989), *Women-Nation-State* (London: Macmillan).

B. Reports and conference papers

Abraham, A. (1987), *Personal Laws in India,* Presented at the Asian Conference on Women, Religion and Family Laws, Bombay, available on file with Akshara Documentation Centre, Mumbai.

Agnes, F. (1988), *Wife Beating – Changes in Social structures Crucial to Combat the Problem* (Paper presented at the National Workshop on "Family Violence Against Females, organized by Integrated Human Development Services Foundation: On file with Akshara).

Aids Bhed Bhav Virodhi Andolan (1991), *Less Than Gay. A Citizens' Report on the Status of Homosexuality in India* (New Delhi: ABVA).

AIDWA (2004), Memorandum on Domestic Violence Act (New Delhi: AIDWA).

Asian Women's Human Rights Council and Vimochana (1995), *A Dreamscape. Redrafting the Platform of Action* (Beijing: AWHRC).

Baxi, U. et. al. (1979), *An Open Letter to the Chief Justice of India, dated 16 September 1979*, on file with Akshara, Mumbai.

Bhrame, S. et. al. (1987), *The Material Basis for Women's Liberation. Against the Current Trend in the Women's Movement* (Bombay: Research Unit for Political Economy).

BJP (1986), Statement by the BJP National Executive (Chandigarh: BJP).

CEDAW (2002), *Report on Indian Women*, www.wcd.nic.in/CEDAW, accessed on 1/02/2006.

Central Social Welfare Board (1996), *Prostitution in Metropolitan Cities of India* (Government of India: New Delhi).

Centre for Society and Secularism (1994), *Impact of Communal Riots on Women* (Bombay: CSS).

Department of Women and Child Development (1998), *Report of the Committee on Prostitution, Child Prostitution and Children of Prostitutes and Plan of Action to Combat Trafficking and Commercial Sexual Exploitation of Women and Children* (New Delhi: Human Resource Development Ministry, Government of India).

Fernandes, G. and Stewart-Ray, C. (nd), *Raids, Rescue, Rehabilitation. The Story of the Mumbai Brothel Raids of 1996–2000* (Mumbai: The College of Social Work, Nirmala Niketan).

Forum Against Oppression of Women (1980), *Draft Resolution on Proposed Changes in the Rape law* (Bombay: FAOW).

Forum Against Oppression of Women (1988), *Letter to Director, Doordarshan,* dated 4 November 1988.

Forum against Oppression of Women (1990), *Moving...but not quite there* (Bombay: FAOW).

Forum Against Oppression of Women (1995), *Visions of Gender Just Realities* (Bombay: FAOW).

Forum Against Oppression of Women et. al. (1994), *Letter by Women's Organisations*, dated 17 April 1995.

Forum Against Oppression of Women (2005), *Concept note for the Feminist Dialogues at Porto Alegre* (Mumbai: FAOW).

Gothoskar, S. (1980) *Politics of Rape* (Bombay: National Conference on Perspectives for Women's Liberation in India).

Government of India (1980), *The Report of the Law Commission. No. 84* (New Delhi, Government of India).

Guha, P. et al. (1974), *Towards Equality, Report of the Committee on the Status of Women in India* (New Delhi: Government of India).

Haksar, N. (nd), *Women and Law, Dominance, Support and the Law: Woman, Family and her Body* (New Delhi: On file with Jagori Documentation Centre).

International Initiative for Justice in Gujarat (2003.) *Threatened Existence. A Feminist Analysis of Genocide in Gujarat.* (Bombay: FAOW).

Joint Committee (1982), *Joint Committee Report on the Bill to amend the Indian Penal Code, 1860, the Criminal Procedure Code, 1973, and the Indian Evidence Act, 1872* (New Delhi: The Gazette of India Extraordinary. Part II, Section II).

Kale, V. (2006), Securing and Safeguarding Rights of Stigmatised through Social and Legal Action, paper presented at Workshop on *Towards a Theory of Law and Social Movements,* organised by the Hauser Centre for Nonprofit Organisations at Harvard University, Bangalore, 26–27 June 2006.

Kamran A. (1994), *The Evolution of Muslim Family Law in India*, Unpublished Paper, on file with Akshara Documentation Centre.

Majlis Manch (1995), *Section 498 A IPC.* (Bombay: Majlis Manch).

Parivarik Surakshya Samiti, *Mission Statement* (New Delhi, 2005).

PUDR (1989), *Inside The Family* (New Delhi: PUDR).

PUDR (1994), *Custodial Rape* (New Delhi: PUDR).

PRISM (2006) *PRISM on the Sexual Assault Bill* (New Delhi: Prism).

RCWS and FAOW (2005), *Working Conditions and Backgrounds of Women Working as Dancers in Dance Bars* (Mumbai: SNDT University).

Sanlaap (1998), *Yet another right. A report on a seminar to discuss different views on legalisation of prostitution* (Kolkata: Sanlaap).

Savara, M. (nd.), *Organising Women in the Unorganised Sector,* Unpublished Paper, on file with Akshara Documentation Centre.

Seshu, M. and Bhonsale, V. (nd), *Imprisoning Womanhood. A Report on the Desertions and Deaths of Women in Sanghli District* (Sanghli: VAMPS).

Shah, C. (2006), Gendered and Sexual: A Queer Feminist look at the Recent Sexual Assault Law Debates, paper presented at Workshop on *Towards a Theory of Law and Social Movements,* organised by the Hauser Centre for Nonprofit Organisations at Harvard University, Bangalore, 26–27 June 2006.

South Asian Women's Groups (1998), *Faultlines* (New Delhi: Jagori).

Vimochana (nd.) *"I cry for help, no one's there..." A Community Campaign to Safeguard a Woman's Right to Live* (Bangalore: Vimochana).

C. Laws and Bills

A Bill to provide for the prevention of bigamous marriages in the State of Maharashtra. LA Bill Number XXXII of 1995. Maharashtra Legislative Secretariat.

Bill Number 162 of 1980, The Gazette of India Extraordinary. Section II, Part 2. 12 August 1980.

Doordarshan, Code for Advertisers. Dated 10 May 1987.

Hindu Adoption and Maintenance Act, 1956.

Hindu Marriage Act, 1955.

Maharashta Protection of Commercial Sex Workers Act, 1994.

National Commission of Women (1992) *Sexual Violence against Women and Children: An Act to Combat Sexual Violence Against Women and Children.* Draft Bill. 1992.

Parsee Marriage and Divorce Act, 1937.

Prevention of Pushing and Forcing a Girl Child into the Flesh Trade and Immoral Traffic Act, 2005.

Section 125 (5) Criminal Procedure Code.

Section 292, Indian Penal Code. Act XLV of 1860.

Section 497, Chapter XX, Indian Penal Code.

Sexual Harassment of Women in their Workplace (Prevention) Bill, 2003.

Special Marriage Act, 1954.

The Protection from Domestic Violence Act 2005. New Delhi, Government of India.

D. Court cases

1986 Cri L J 2087. (Punjab and Haryana High Court): 2092

AIR 1980. SCC 249, 1980 Cri L J. 8.

Arab Ahemadhia Abdulla v. Arab Bail Mohmuna Saiyadbhai. AIR 1988 Gujarat 141.

Bai Tahira v. Ali Hussein Fissalli Chothia and Another. AIR 1979. SC 362.

In the Supreme Court of India. Criminal Original Jurisdiction. Writ Petition (Criminal) Number 421 of 1989.

Inder Raj Malik and Others v. Mrs. Sunita Malik. 1986 Cri L J 1510.

Krishnalal v. State of Haryana. AIR 1980. SCC 1252.

Latifi and Khan v. The Union of India. In The Supreme Court of India. Public Interest Jurisdiction. Writ Petition No. 868 of 1986. In The Matter of the Muslim Women Protection of Rights upon Divorce Act, 1986.

Mahila Sanyukta Morcha v. Premchand and Others, In the Supreme Court of India. Criminal Appellate Jurisdiction. Review Petition of 1989 in the Special Leave Petition. (Cal.) Numbers 800–801 of 1996.

Mohommed Ahmed Khan v. Shah Bano Begum and Others. AIR 1985. SC 945.

Prem Chand and Another v. The State of Haryana. 1989 Cri L J 1246.

Rafiq v. State of Uttar Pradesh. 1980. Cri L J 1344.

Rahmatullah v. State of UP, Khatoonisa V. State of UP. AIR 1993. Judgment dated 4 April 1993.

Raj Kapoor v. State (Delhi Administration) AIR 1980. SC 258.

Sarla Mudgal and Others v. the Union of India and Others. II 1995. DMC 351 (SC).

Saroj Rani v. Sudarshan Kumar Chadda. AIR 1984. SC 1562.

Shahnaz Shaikh v. The Union of India and Adbul Rab Kavish. Civil Writ Petition No. 32 of 1983. In the matter of Article 32 of the Constitution of India and In the matter of Article 14, 15. 25 and 26 of the Constitution of India and In the matter of the Muslim Personal Law. In the Supreme Court of India. Civil Original Jurisdiction.

Shahzadi Begum v. Mohommad Abdul Gaffar. 1981. Cri L J 1532.

Shanti v. State of Haryana. AIR 1991. SC 1226.

Sharad Birdhichand Sarda v. State of Maharashtra. AIR 1984 SC 1622.

Smt. Sarla Prabhakar Wagmare v. State of Maharashtra and Others. 1990 Cri L J 407.

Smt. Shanta Devi v. Raghav Prakash. AIR 1986. Raj 13.

Smt. Tirath Kaur v. Kirpal Singh. AIR 1964. Punjab 28.

Soumitra Vishnu v. Union of India. AIR 1985 SCC 1618.

State of Maharashtra v. Prakash and Another. 1922. Cri L J 1984.

State of Maharasthra v. Chandraprakash Kewalchand Jain with Stree Atyachar Virodhi Parishad v. Chandraprakash Kewalchand Jain. January 1990. Cri L J 889.

T Sareetha v. T Venkatasubbaih. AIR 1983. AP 356.

Vincent Adolf Gondinho v. June Beatrice Rana Gondinho. MLJ 1984: 926–30.

Vishakha and Anrs. v. Union of India, AIR 1997 SC 3011.

Wazir Chand v. State of Haryana. AIR 1989. SC 378.

E. Legislative Debates

Lok Sabha Debates (1976a), Fifth Series, Volume LX, n. 28. 28 April 1976.

Lok Sabha Debates (1976b), Volume LX, n. 32, 20 May 1976, 160–161.

Lok Sabha Debates (1976c), Volume LX, n. 33, 21 May 1976, 8–90.

Lok Sabha Debates (1976d), Volume LX, n. 35, 24 May 1976, 8–38.

Lok Sabha Debates (1980a), Seventh Series. Volume V. n. 13, 26 June 1980, 744–50.

Lok Sabha Debates (1980b), Volume V. n.16: 235, n.17, 2 July 1980, 251– 60.

Lok Sabha Debates (1980c), Volume V. n. 18, 4 July 1980, 454– 524.

Lok Sabha Debates (1981), Volume 29, n. 4 and 5, 368–498.

Lok Sabha Debates (1982), Volume 30, n. 1, 305–306.

Lok Sabha Debates (1982), Volume 39, n.6–10, 415–55.

Lok Sabha Debates (1983a), Volume 42, n.1, 15 July 1983, 415–474.

Lok Sabha Debates (1983b) Volume 42, n.1, 21 November 1983, 417–550.

Lok Sabha Debates (1983c) Volume 42, n.2, 1 December 1983, 367–550.

Lok Sabha Debates (1983d) Volume 42, n.3, 21 December 1983: 367–550.

Lok Sabha Debates (1984), Vol. 45, 5 April 1983, 328–371.

Lok Sabha Debates (1986a), 5 May 1986, 239–444.

Lok Sabha Debates (1986b), Volume LXX, 22 August 1986, 158–200.

Index